Command Post Leadership

Command Post Leadership: A Fieldbook for Building Trust, Plans, and Teams

Craig Oglesby

Andrew Partin

Outsiders Group Publishing

Command Post Leadership: A Fieldbook for Building Trust, Plans, and Teams

Published by Outsiders Group Publishing
An imprint of Outsiders Group LLC
Atlanta, GA
www.outsiders-group.com

All rights reserved. No part of this publication may be reproduced, distributed, or transmitted in any form or by any means—including photocopying, recording, or other electronic or mechanical methods-without the prior written permission of the publisher, except in the case of brief quotations embodied in critical reviews and certain other noncommercial uses permitted by copyright law.

For permission requests, write to:

Permissions Department
Outsiders Group Publishing
PO Box A
Toccoa GA 30577

ISBN: 9798993575902

Library of Congress Control Number: 2025922572

Printed in the United States of America

DEDICATION

To the men and women we had the honor to lead, who taught us what leadership really means. Without you, this book wouldn't exist. And without your trust, loyalty, and love, we wouldn't be the leaders or the men we are today.

To our wives and children who've endured every deployment, detour, debrief, and move; to our dogs, who listened without judgment and probably understood more than we realized.

To the leaders who led us, trained us, challenged us, and occasionally smoked us, you showed us what right looks like (and sometimes what it doesn't). We learned from all of it. The lessons you passed down shaped our own approach to leadership, and your example still echoes in our decisions today.

With gratitude and respect, we acknowledge our first Cohort, The 2006 Auburn University Army ROTC Commissioning Class.

These stories are told from our recollections, drawn from experiences that shaped us over the past two decades. While we've done our best to represent the events truthfully, some details may be incomplete, out of sequence, or colored by the passage of time. Any errors or oversights are unintentional and simply a reflection of memory, not a deliberate attempt to mislead. Our goal is to share meaningful lessons and authentic reflections, even if the exact dialogue or timeline isn't perfect.

Free Templates and Resources
www.outsiders-group.com/free-resources

Hear more from Craig and Andrew on The Command Post Cohort podcast, available anywhere you listen to podcasts.

To reach out to us regarding consulting and in-person training, you can find more information at
www.outsiders-group.com

Contents

How to Use This Book

This book is a workshop in a cover, not just something to read and shelve. It is intended to be a tool for use when you are actively working on projects, as well as a reference for improving your organization. Start by skimming a chapter to get the story and the core idea, then come back and *do* the work: use the templates and run one framework against a real problem you are facing this week. Treat the narrative stories (the personal examples and "Craig/Andrew" perspectives) as case studies — read them for context, then extract the practical steps you can mirror or adapt. Use the templates as living tools: print one, fill it out in a meeting, share it with your team, and save the next version so you can track progress. Pace yourself, one chapter + one applied exercise per week builds momentum without burnout. Keep an "action log" (notebook or digital) where you write what you tried, what changed, and the next small experiment. The goal is simple: move ideas into repeatable practice, so stories become habits and templates become outcomes.

We have also added leader reflection questions and team discussion prompts to the end of each chapter. These are intended to help you facilitate conversations with your team to continuously improve your organization. They can also be used for self-reflection or discussing challenges and opportunities with your peers.

Leadership in Brief
Key Principles of this book

Intent drives adaptability and alignment.

When teams know the purpose and end state, they can act boldly, even in chaos, without waiting for permission.

Clear standards build trust. Trust builds teams. Teams win.

Leaders must clearly communicate standards. Clarity prevents confusion, resentment, and failure.

Explain the "why," adapt the "how."

Purposeful communication explains the intent and empowers your team to solve the problems.

Purpose is your leadership compass.

When purpose is clear, decisions get easier, motivation stays strong, and teams move as one.

A plan is a promise to your team.

Planning builds trust. It shows your team you care enough to prepare them, and equips them to respond when conditions change.

Leaders make decisions, not excuses.

Avoiding decisions paralyzes teams. Even imperfect decisions move organizations forward.

Risk hides in the things we overlook.

The obvious threats rarely sink the mission; it is the missed details and complacency that do. Stay vigilant.

Great leaders don't give all the answers; they ask better questions.

Coaching is not about control. It is about guiding people to discover their own solutions and grow through the process.

Move toward the storm.

Avoidance of conflict erodes trust. Addressing conflict quickly and constructively demonstrates strength and care.

You don't rise to the occasion; you fall to the level of your training.

Great outcomes come from consistent reps. Train hard, train real, and make training count.

Change is the environment, not the exception.

Leaders who expect stability are always behind. Embrace change as the normal terrain of leadership. This will keep your organization ahead of its competitors.

The Command Post Leadership System

The primary objective of leadership is trust.
Everything else a leader does either builds it or quietly erodes it. Most leadership models treat trust as a personality trait or an outcome of good intentions. Charisma, authenticity, or "being yourself" are often offered as the solution. But trust does not scale on personality alone. And it does not survive pressure without structure. Trust is built and sustained through consistent leader behavior over time. That is the purpose of the Command Post Leadership System.

What This System Is (and What It Is Not)

The Command Post Leadership System is not a motivational philosophy. It is not a rigid checklist. And it is not dependent on rank, title, or authority.

It is a practical, repeatable approach leaders use to intentionally build trust, especially when conditions are uncertain, time is limited, or the stakes are high. This system focuses on how leaders behave, not how they want to be perceived.

How Trust Is Built

Trust is not demanded; it is earned through consistency. The Command Post Leadership System identifies five leadership mechanisms that, when applied deliberately, produce trust as an outcome:

Standards → Communication → Decision-Making → Planning → Presence

Applied consistently. Reviewed continuously.

These mechanisms work together as a system. Neglect one, and trust weakens. Apply them with discipline, and trust compounds.

The Five Trust-Building Mechanisms

1. Standards

Trust begins with clarity.

Standards define what "right" looks like, what is non-negotiable and where judgment and initiative are expected. When standards are clear and consistently enforced, teams stop guessing. They trust the system—not personalities, moods, or favoritism.

Leadership Question:
What does right look like, and do people see it modeled consistently?

Trust Built Through:
Predictability · Fairness · Accountability without fear

2. Communication

Trust requires shared understanding. Communication is not volume; it is clarity and consistency.

Effective leaders communicate purpose, decisions, and changes in whatever way is necessary to ensure they are understood. They confirm understanding rather than assuming, and reduce ambiguity before it becomes friction.

Leadership Question:
Do people understand the why, not just the what?

Trust Built Through:
Reduced confusion · Fewer assumptions · Stronger alignment

3. Decision-Making

Trust grows when decisions are timely and transparent.

Leaders build trust by clarifying who decides what and explaining the rationale when it matters. Slow, hidden, or inconsistent decisions create hesitation. Clear decision authority creates confidence.

Leadership Question:
Are decisions being made at the right level, at the right speed?

Trust Built Through:
Empowerment · Initiative · Confidence in leadership

4. Planning

Trust is strengthened when leaders think ahead. Planning builds trust by demonstrating foresight, discipline, and respect for people's time and effort

Good plans do not predict the future. They prepare teams to adapt together.

Leadership Question:
Have we thought this through well enough to execute with confidence?

Trust Built Through:
Reduced chaos · Better coordination · Shared direction

5. Presence

Trust is personal.

Presence is how leaders show up under pressure, during conflict, and when things go wrong. Leaders are always the example, especially when they are not speaking.

Leadership Question:
What do my actions signal when it matters most?

Trust Built Through:
Psychological safety · Credibility · Commitment

The System in Practice

The Command Post Leadership System is cyclical, not linear.

Leaders continually set standards, communicate with intent, make decisions, and plans to enable their team to achieve goals. Each cycle either strengthens trust or weakens it. There is no neutral ground.

You do not need to change who you are to build trust. You need to change how deliberately you lead. Leaders do not demand trust. They earn it through standards, clarity, and consistent behavior.

Introduction:

Where It All Began — High Standards, Real Conversations, and the Auburn Cohort

Before we ever stepped into combat zones or boardrooms, before we commanded troops or consulted executives, we were two young college students learning the fundamentals of leadership in Auburn, Alabama. Our leadership foundation began with our first Army ROTC cohort.

Our class came together in 2002, part of a unique generation of cadets. Our time in ROTC began just after 9/11. The country was at war, and everyone in the program understood what they were signing up for. Our cohort was forged in those uncertain times. Not by accident, but by choice. That choice was a decision to be leaders heading into war. It required high standards, relentless training, and authentic leadership.

Our development in ROTC came in two distinct phases. The first two years introduced us to the basics: how to wear a uniform, use a compass, and lead a simple formation. It was structured, traditional, and discipline focused. Our first Professor of Military Science (PMS) came from an armor background, and he taught us the textbook fundamentals of leadership: standards, discipline, and proper planning.

In our junior year, we got a new PMS, a Special Forces officer who shifted the tone. It was no longer just about what leadership looked like; it became about how it felt. He emphasized the weight of responsibility, the value of trust, and the importance of doing more than just meeting expectations. And that is when our cohort really came together. Everything changed when the standards went from passing to excelling. The Army's requirement to pass the land navigation test was to find 5 of 8 points during the day and 3 of 5 at night. That wasn't good enough for us. Our standard became 8 of 8 and 5 of 5. Our cadre demanded it, but we held each other to it.

Field Takeaway (Andrew): "Leadership doesn't start when you're in charge—it starts when you hold yourself and your peers to a higher standard."

We didn't get there overnight. It was repetition. We spent almost every weekend, unless Auburn had a home football game, in the woods of the Tuskegee National Forest. Day and night, rain or shine, we trained. We failed early and learned this would not come easily. We got better. We worked together. We made sure no one fell short. Not because we were told to, but because we didn't want to let each other down.

One of the biggest lessons we took from Auburn ROTC wasn't just how to complete a task. It was about being accountable for the people around you. You couldn't say "that's their problem." If someone on your team failed, it was your problem too. We learned that, as leaders, we were responsible not only for our own behavior but also for shaping the behavior of our team members.

That's what leadership really is. It's not the big motivational speeches. It's the small, consistent, intentional moments that shape how we lead and how others grow under our leadership.

We didn't realize it then, but Auburn ROTC wasn't just teaching us how to wear the uniform. It was giving us a framework for leadership that we still use today:

- Set the standard high.
- Train people thoroughly and give them chances to fail forward.
- Hold your peers accountable and support them when they stumble.
- Have real conversations, one-on-one, with authenticity and intent.
- Recognize that leadership is a team sport.

Leadership in Action: Craig- Real Leadership is Personal

There's a training exercise that still stands out in my memory — not because everything went perfectly, but because of what I learned afterward.

We were running a multi-school exercise, moving through scenarios designed to test leadership under pressure. The pace was fast, expectations were high, and everyone knew they were being evaluated. I was serving as the squad leader, responsible for coordinating the team and ensuring we executed effectively.

From my perspective, things were going well. We moved efficiently. We hit most of our objectives. When the exercise wrapped up, I felt confident. The feedback from evaluators suggested I had performed well overall, and for a moment, I allowed myself to feel satisfied.

As the group began to disperse, one of the instructors approached me. "Walk with me for a minute," he said.

We stepped off to the side, away from the rest of the platoon. There was no audience, no raised voices — just a calm, direct presence. He looked at me and asked, "Why did you let them do so poorly?" The question caught me off guard.

My first instinct was defensive. I thought, Let them? I had focused on my responsibilities. I had made the right decisions. We had achieved our mission. Wasn't that the goal? I started to respond, already forming explanations in my mind. "Well, sergeant, I was focused on—" He raised a hand slightly, not dismissive, just steady.

"I'm not asking what they did wrong," he said. "I'm asking why you let it happen."

The words landed differently the second time.

> *In that moment, I realized he wasn't criticizing my performance as much as reframing my understanding of leadership. I had been measuring success by my individual evaluation, not by the growth and performance of the people I was responsible for.*
>
> *"If they're on your team," he continued, "and they're failing — that's your responsibility." He was showing me that there was a lot more to leadership than just being a good individual performer.*
>
> *There was no anger in his tone. No public correction. Just clarity.*
>
> *We stood there quietly for a moment while I processed what he had said. The exercise replayed in my mind — moments when I had noticed others struggle but chose to push forward rather than slow down and coach. Times when I assumed my performance would overcome others' weaknesses rather than address them directly.*
>
> *I had led the mission. But I hadn't fully led the people.*
>
> *That conversation didn't happen in front of the entire company. It wasn't part of a formal briefing or a dramatic leadership speech. It was a quiet, one-on-one exchange — authentic, respectful, and focused on growth rather than embarrassment.*
>
> *And it changed how I thought about leadership.*
>
> *I realized that leadership isn't measured by whether you personally succeed. It's measured by whether the people you lead improve because you were there.*

We saw how repetition builds skills and confidence. We learned that leadership requires you to know your people, not just their strengths, but their struggles, their motivations, and their goals.

Our cohort didn't just survive Auburn ROTC; we thrived. We earned active duty slots in competitive branches. We deployed. We commanded. Later, we applied those same lessons to build businesses, lead teams, and teach others.

That's why our podcast is called *Command Post Cohort*. Because everything we do now started with that group. That team and culture built us into young leaders, starting a lifelong journey.

This isn't a story about nostalgia. It's a blueprint for leaders. In every chapter that follows, we will draw from those lessons learned in the woods, tested in war, and applied in life.

Welcome to *The Cohort*.

"A leader is responsible for everything their unit does or fails to do." That truth started at Auburn, and it never stopped being true.

Leader Reflection Questions:

1. What foundational experiences shaped your leadership expectations?
2. Are you setting the minimum standard, or pushing your team to the exceptional?

Team Discussion Prompts:

1. What are we doing regularly that deserves a higher standard? and how can we build that together?
2. Are we holding each other accountable?

Chapter One

Trust, Tasks, and Purpose: Why Clarity Builds Confidence

Purpose is one of the most powerful tools a leader can wield. In our military careers and business ventures, we've consistently seen how clarity of purpose transforms compliance into commitment, task execution into mission success, and subordinates into empowered teammates. Whether leading soldiers in Afghanistan or managing teams in complex environments, the most successful outcomes stem from a shared understanding of the "why" behind the work.

Should Leaders Always Explain the Purpose?

At first glance, explaining the purpose behind every task may seem time-consuming. Leaders often operate in high-tempo environments where efficiency and speed are prized, and the instinct to "just get it done" is strong. But skipping the explanation undermines more than we realize. When people don't understand the reasoning behind a decision or task, they're more likely to resist it, execute it poorly, or miss opportunities for improvement.

That's not to say every single instruction requires a dissertation. Telling someone to clean their workspace may not require an executive summary on organizational hygiene. But when introducing major changes like a new payroll system, a shift in strategic focus, or a reorganization of team structure, the "why" is essential.

> ## Leadership in Action: Craig- Compliance to Commitment
>
> *During my time as a company commander of a basic training unit, I was responsible for leading and training hundreds of new soldiers. At first glance, you might assume that such an environment would run on blind obedience. But I quickly learned that the best soldiers weren't the ones who just followed orders—they were the ones who understood them.*
>
> *Even in a rigid training environment, my goal wasn't to produce order-followers. I wanted to develop thinkers. When soldiers grasped the purpose behind their actions, they brought far more value to the mission.*
>
> *I've found the same principle holds true in business. When a team understands the deeper purpose behind a project—how it aligns with the company's mission, how it affects the customer, and how it connects with other departments—they perform at a higher level. They don't just complete tasks. They solve problems, create value, and adapt with intent.*

When people understand the reason behind the task, they become partners in the outcome. They take ownership, think critically, and most importantly, trust their leader. If you've consistently communicated purpose, your team will be far more responsive in situations where you must act quickly and can't afford a detailed explanation. Explaining the rationale for tasks or projects helps your team deliver better outcomes by providing a clearer understanding of the situation. It empowers them to go far beyond what they were told.

Micromanagement kills creativity and stalls progress. When we lead with empowered intent, we give ourselves space to focus on strategic problems, external coordination, and future planning, the work that truly drives long-term success.

Leadership in Action: Andrew- Intent and Initiative

During my time at Fort Benning, I brought on a civilian hire I'd worked with before. I saw his work and knew he was smart and capable.

I took some time after I hired him to set expectations and let him know what I expected of him and what he could expect of me. We were working on a big project that required us to work constantly with many other offices across the Army, often with little notice. It was often detailed work that required precision execution and disciplined attention to detail.

Initially, he would walk into my office several times a day, hesitant to take action or extend discussions with external agencies without my express permission. One afternoon, he came into my office, "Sir, I drafted the changes we discussed. Should I shoot it over to the other branch and the medics?"

Somewhat frustrated but joking, I said, "I didn't hire you so that I could do more work. Look, we've discussed the changes, you know my intent. If a decision aligns with that goal, you have my permission to make it. Don't ask me what to do—tell me what you've done."

He looked like a mix of stunned, relieved, and terrified. A smile slowly spread across his face. He said, "Ok, Sir. I got you" and turned around and walked out excitedly. The problem wasn't his ability but his individual risk calculation of stepping outside of my expectations.

Once I clarified to him that I trusted him to act within my guidance, he felt free to act. I didn't hear from him for two days.

> *At the end of the second day, he came to me and said, "I sent what we discussed to the medics and they disagreed. So I worked with the other branch to come to a compromise with them. We all came to a solution, and I just need your signature before I take it to the Director."*
>
> *"Yes! Exactly!" I exclaimed. "This is why I hired you." His taking those actions allowed me to work on other projects and to influence other leaders to advance our work. I signed the document and said, "Go on in there, he's expecting you."*
>
> *As leaders, we don't just delegate tasks; we delegate the authority to execute based on a shared purpose.*

Understanding the Organization's Purpose—Not Just Your Own

Leaders must not only understand their personal or departmental purpose, but also how that purpose fits into the larger enterprise. A manufacturing manager may optimize for speed or cost, but if those decisions result in poor product quality or burdensome issues for downstream teams, they have failed the organization even if their local metrics look great.

Purpose shouldn't be siloed. If you do not understand how your work affects marketing, logistics, finance, and ultimately the customer, you're at risk of making short-term decisions that create long-term problems.

One of the best illustrations of this came from a manufacturing case study we discussed in business school. A division improved its production metrics by using lower-cost materials, only to find that these parts failed more often, resulting in more warranty claims and damage to the brand's reputation. When decisions are made without understanding the larger purpose, everyone loses.

The Drill Bit Is Not the Goal

In business, understanding purpose also means recognizing what customers genuinely want. As the saying goes, no one buys a half-inch drill bit because they want one—they want a half-inch hole. If your company sells drill bits, your job is not just to manufacture a product; it is to deliver a solution. That subtle shift in mindset from selling products to solving problems clarifies decision-making, improves customer satisfaction, and fosters innovation.

When organizations embrace this perspective, they start asking better questions: *What is the customer really trying to accomplish? What frustrations can we remove? How can we make their success easier, faster, or more enjoyable?* A company focused on selling drill bits might stop at improving materials or packaging. A company focused on delivering holes, however, might pioneer cordless drills, laser guides, or even entirely new fastening systems. One mindset protects market share; the other expands it.

For leaders, this principle goes beyond product design it influences culture and strategy. Teams that are aligned around solving problems are more adaptable, more collaborative, and more motivated because they see how their work directly connects to customer outcomes. When customers feel understood and served at a deeper level, loyalty grows, referrals spread, and innovation becomes part of the organization's identity.

Ultimately, purpose is not about what you make, it's about the difference you make. Leaders who consistently frame decisions through the lens of customer outcomes will build organizations that stay relevant, resilient, and trusted, even as markets and technologies change.

Mission Command: Leadership Through Intent

In the early 2000s, the U.S. Army shifted from a leadership model based on *command and control* to one called *mission command*. This change wasn't just doctrinal; it was also philosophical. (Department of the Army 2019)

Command and control emphasized strict procedures and top-down direction. Mission command emphasized trust, intent, and decentralized decision-making. It asked a simple question: "Did the mission get accomplished?" not "Did you follow the steps in the right order?" This approach was forged in the fires of counterinsurgency operations, where rigid plans quickly broke down and junior leaders had to make life-or-death decisions with limited guidance. Leaders provided their intent and boundaries, then trusted their teams to figure out the rest. It was no longer a question of doing what you were told; it was the question of whether you solved the problem you were given. There was no longer a step by step process to complete and hope it worked but a focus on the outcomes achieved.

The old system relied on obedience, and that was the main measure of success. If you did what you were told, then that's all you could do. However, in the mission command philosophy, it was more about how the leaders adapted to the situation and achieved the solution their leaders were seeking. The main requirement to be able to ensure your solution to the problem would be considered successful was to understand the purpose behind what task you had been given.

For example, if your unit was tasked with destroying a bridge to prevent the enemy from moving to the other side of the river. No one cared if you destroyed the bridge if the enemy still made it across the river. The purpose of preventing enemy movement across the river failed, so the destroyed bridge was unsuccessful. The outcomes and results are more important than the steps involved.

Leadership is not a checklist—it's a mindset built on trust, clarity, and intent.

Purpose Builds Trust. Trust Builds Teams.

Purpose isn't just a communication tool. It's a trust-building tool. Every time you explain the why, follow through, or support your people, you're making a deposit in the trust bank. One day, you'll need to make a withdrawal. You'll need them to act fast, improvise, or execute with little guidance. Whether they trust you in that moment depends on the trust you've built beforehand.

Understanding purpose also helps people withstand change. If a team knows why the company is pivoting, they're more likely to embrace it. If they don't, resistance builds. Resistance is a symptom of poor communication and low trust, not of poor employees.

> ## *Leadership in Action: Andrew- Mission Command*
>
> *One experience that stands out to me was when I had a platoon dispatched to shut down a remote base in Afghanistan. We had very little notice and even less information. The leader on the ground had to make decisions quickly and independently. There was no script to follow—success depended on understanding the mission, adapting in real time, and trusting the team to execute.*
>
> *That's the essence of mission command: clear intent, empowered execution, and trust. I've seen how powerful that same approach is in business. When leaders provide clarity and trust their teams to figure out the "how," great things happen—even in uncertain conditions.*

Commander's Intent: Clarity, Focus, and Initiative

Commander's Intent (Department of the Army 2019) is a critical leadership tool that communicates more than just what needs to be done, it communicates *why* it needs to be done and *what success looks like*. It bridges the gap between high-level strategy and on-the-ground execution by outlining three essential elements: purpose, key tasks, and the desired end state.

The **purpose** explains *why* the mission or objective matters. It gives meaning to the work and helps align individual effort with the broader mission. Without understanding the purpose, teams may complete tasks without knowing how they contribute to the bigger picture, leading to inefficiency or misaligned effort.

The **key tasks** are the non-negotiable actions that must be accomplished for the mission to succeed. These guide teams on where to focus their energy, even when the environment changes. In both military and business settings, key tasks ensure the team stays aligned when executing under pressure.

The **desired end state** paints a clear picture of what success looks like. This allows team members to adapt in real-time without needing constant oversight. Commander's Intent enables speed, agility, and intelligent initiative because everyone knows what outcome they're trying to achieve. This becomes especially valuable in dynamic environments. Too often, success is not clearly defined, and teams can't achieve what they don't understand.

In business, this framework is just as vital as it is in combat. When a project leader clearly articulates the intent behind a product launch, a sales campaign, or a crisis response plan, teams are better equipped to operate independently and make decisions that support the overall goal. Rather than getting stuck waiting for direction, empowered teams can move faster, solve problems on the fly, and stay aligned with the organization's priorities.

Commander's Intent is ultimately about trust and clarity. It allows leaders to step back from micromanaging and focus on higher-level strategy while empowering their teams to execute with confidence, creativity, and purpose—whether in the field or the boardroom. *(Checkout our template on page 19 to help create your own leader's intent)*

From the battlefield to the boardroom, the lesson is clear: purpose builds trust. Whether you're leading a squad of soldiers, a department of professionals, or an entire enterprise—clarity of purpose creates alignment, trust, and action. Leaders who explain why, lead with intent, and cultivate trust build teams that think, act, and perform. That's leadership at its highest form.

Key Principle: Intent drives adaptability and alignment.

When teams know the purpose and end state, they can act boldly, even in chaos, without waiting for permission.

Leader Reflection Questions:

1. When was the last time I clearly explained the "why" behind a task or initiative? What was the outcome?
2. Do I trust my team enough to make decisions without me, or do I default to micromanagement? Why?
3. Have I invested enough in trust-building to expect initiative in moments of ambiguity or urgency?
4. How well have I communicated my intent and expectations for recent projects or priorities?
5. Are there key tasks in my organization that are being completed without clarity on the larger mission or impact?

Team Discussion Prompts:

1. What does "purpose" mean in our team's context—and do we all agree on what it is?
2. How would you describe our version of Commander's Intent? Do we know the mission, key tasks, and end state?
3. Think of a recent project—did we understand the "why" behind what we were doing, or were we just checking boxes?
4. Are there tasks or roles on our team that feel disconnected from our bigger purpose? How can we fix that?
5. If we had to operate for a week without direction from senior leaders, what would we focus on, and why?

Business Leader's Intent Template

Use this document to clarify the purpose and end-state of a mission-critical business effort. It enables decentralized decision-making while keeping everyone aligned.

1. Purpose (Why)

State the deeper reason for the initiative beyond just task completion. What larger goal or problem are we addressing? *"Why are we doing this? What strategic objective does this support?"*

____

____

2. Key Tasks (What Must Be Done)

List the critical activities or outcomes that must occur to achieve the intent. These are non-negotiables even if the plan changes. *"What absolutely must happen to be successful, regardless of the approach?"*

____

____

3. End-State (What Success Looks Like)

Describe the desired conditions at the conclusion of the effort. This includes qualitative and quantitative indicators. *"How will we know we've succeeded? What should the team, client, or customer experience at the end?"*

____

____

Example 1: Business Leader's Intent –

Internal Process Improvement Initiative (Reducing Invoice Processing Time)

1. Purpose (Why)

Our current invoice processing time is 12 days, which creates bottlenecks in vendor relationships and cash flow management. This initiative aims to streamline the process to under five days by standardizing workflows and automating manual steps.

2. Key Tasks (What Must Be Done)

- Map out the current invoice process and identify delays.
- Implement a new digital invoice tracking system.
- Train all finance and operations staff on the new workflow.
- Pilot the new process with 3 vendors before full rollout.
- Create dashboards to track performance post-implementation.

3. End-State (What Success Looks Like)

Within 60 days, average invoice processing time is reduced to 5 days or fewer, staff report improved workflow clarity, and vendor satisfaction increases based on post-implementation feedback.

Example 2: Business Leader's Intent –

Opening a New Regional Office

1. **Purpose (Why)**

We are opening a new regional office in Nashville to expand our physical presence in the Southeast, improve client service response times, and tap into a growing talent pool for long-term scalability. This supports our 3-year strategic growth initiative.

2. **Key Tasks (What Must Be Done)**

- Secure office lease and complete setup by September 15.
- Hire and onboard five new staff members by October 1.
- Host a ribbon-cutting event with local stakeholders and media.
- Transition three major clients to local account teams by October 15.
- Establish operational systems (IT, payroll, HR support) that match HQ standards.

3. **End-State (What Success Looks Like)**

By the end of Q4, the Nashville office is fully operational, delivering seamless client service with a local team, maintaining brand consistency, and actively contributing to regional sales goals with 3+ new customers.

Example 3: Business Leader's Intent –

New Software Launch

1. Purpose (Why)

To successfully launch our new project management software, targeting small and mid-sized businesses overwhelmed by complex tools. This launch is part of our strategy to diversify revenue and position ourselves as a customer-focused alternative in the SaaS market.

2. Key Tasks (What Must Be Done)

- Complete beta testing with a 95% satisfaction rate by July 15.
- Ensure customer support and sales staff are trained on the new software before launch.
- Deploy website, pricing page, and onboarding sequence by July 25.
- Reach 1,000 trial sign-ups within the first 30 days post-launch.
- Launch coordinated marketing campaign (email, social, PR) on July 26.

3. End-State (What Success Looks Like)

By August 31, our software is publicly available, our systems are stable, onboarding works seamlessly, and we've generated positive customer feedback, 1,000+ sign-ups, and 5+ early customer testimonials.

Chapter Two

Using Standards to Enhance Trust and Performance in Teams

Clearly defined standards, when communicated and upheld, serve as a cornerstone for leadership, accountability, and team performance. Rather than being a rigid constraint, standards should be viewed as a framework that enables autonomy, builds trust, and creates alignment across any organization.

Standards Aren't the Enemy

"Standards" often carry negative baggage. People may hear the word and think of micromanagement, rigid quotas, or performance reviews. But properly implemented standards are not about control; they are about clarity. They remove ambiguity, align expectations, and create the conditions for empowered decision-making.

Standards aren't just for subordinates, they apply to leaders to. A good standard is transparent, shared, and mutually enforced across the team. If there's a standard for performance on your team, you as the leader, are held accountable to that same standard or in most cases one higher.

Leaders are constantly under pressure to make decisions quickly and effectively. However, it can be difficult to make the best decisions without the right information. This is where standards can be a critical part of success.

Leadership in Action: Craig- Known vs. Assumed Standards

One of the clearest failures in leadership is expecting people to meet unspoken standards. I saw this firsthand during my time working in a fire department, where traditions often carried more weight than written policy—even when no one ever explained them aloud.

At our station, there was an unwritten expectation that the newest member would help clean up after meals. It wasn't a punishment or a rigid rule — just part of how we shared responsibility and learned to support each other. The problem was that no one had ever formally said it.

That evening started like any other shift. Dinner was loud and relaxed, stories bouncing around the table as people finally slowed down after a busy day. When the meal wrapped up, plates were stacked, chairs pushed back, and the crew drifted out of the kitchen, conversations continuing into the dayroom.

A few minutes later, someone glanced back toward the sink.

It was still full. "Where's the new guy?" one of the senior firefighters asked.

Someone shrugged. "Probably on his phone."

The assumption spread quickly — quiet frustration, a few sideways comments, the kind that builds before anyone actually knows what's going on.

What no one saw was the recruit out in the apparatus bay, sleeves rolled up, wiping down equipment and reorganizing tools left out from the last call. He wasn't avoiding work — he was doing what made sense to him. He saw gear out of place and assumed that was the priority.

When one of the senior guys finally walked toward the bay, his tone carried irritation.

"You going to help with anything tonight?" he called out.

The recruit looked up, surprised. "I thought I was," he said, gesturing toward the equipment. "I figured this needed to be done."

The tension shifted immediately. He wasn't being lazy. He wasn't checked out. He just didn't know the expectation.

I stepped in before it escalated.

"Hey," I said, keeping my voice calm. "Around here, after dinner we usually all jump in and knock out the kitchen together. Come help me for a few minutes."

He nodded right away. "Oh — yeah. Nobody told me that. I thought everyone just handled their own stuff."

"Fair enough," I said. "Now you know."

We walked back toward the kitchen together, and I grabbed a towel while he moved to the sink. Within minutes we were joking with the rest of the crew, the tension gone as quickly as it had appeared. The problem had never been effort. It wasn't attitude. It was clarity.

That moment stayed with me because it revealed something simple but powerful: leaders don't get to be frustrated when someone fails to meet a standard that was never communicated. Expectations that live only in tradition or assumption aren't leadership — they're guesswork.

If our people don't know what's expected of them, that's not their failure. It's ours.

Standards are a set of rules or guidelines that define what is expected in a given situation. They can be used to improve decision-making by providing a framework for evaluating options and making choices.

When standards are clear and well-defined, they can help leaders to delegate decisions to others. This can free up leaders' time to focus on more strategic tasks. It can also help to improve morale and productivity, as employees feel more empowered to make decisions that affect their work.

There are three ways that standards can enable the delegation of decisions:

1. **Provide a framework for decision-making**. When standards are clear and well-defined, they provide a framework for evaluating options and making choices. This can help leaders to make sound decisions more quickly and easily. If there are standards in place, it takes the guesswork out of the hands of a front-line supervisor wondering what the boss would prefer they do. When the team knows what is expected, it takes the ambiguity out of a lot of the decisions leaders must make. A lot of decisions boil down to whether the action meets the standard or not, creating a simple decision in an otherwise difficult environment.

2. **Encourage accountability**. When standards are in place, there is a clear expectation of what is acceptable performance. This can help to encourage accountability and ensure that everyone is working towards the same goals. Performance can easily be objectively quantified and assessed when there are published standards in an organization. It alleviates the fear that someone will think you are playing favorites when there is a clear standard to hold the entire team to.

3. **Improve communication**. Standards can help to improve communication by providing a common language for discussing performance and expectations. This can help to break down silos and promote collaboration. This also keeps senior leaders free to focus on other issues, when midlevel leaders can effectively communicate with their teams and cross-collaborate with others, operating under clear standards

and expectations. A shared understanding of expectations prevents a multitude of questions that can easily lead to micromanagement.

Left and Right Limits: Empowerment Through Clarity

Standards can act as "left and right limits"— when a Soldier is given a position to defend, they are given an azimuth on their compass to their approximate "10 and 2" as on a clock face, and they are responsible for observing any activity between those two points. Soldiers are trained to ensure their range card depicts this area of responsibility, and they become familiar with what is inside it. They are responsible for potential enemies in that area and have the freedom to decide how to engage with their weapon depending on the situation.

(picture below of a range card with left and right limits)

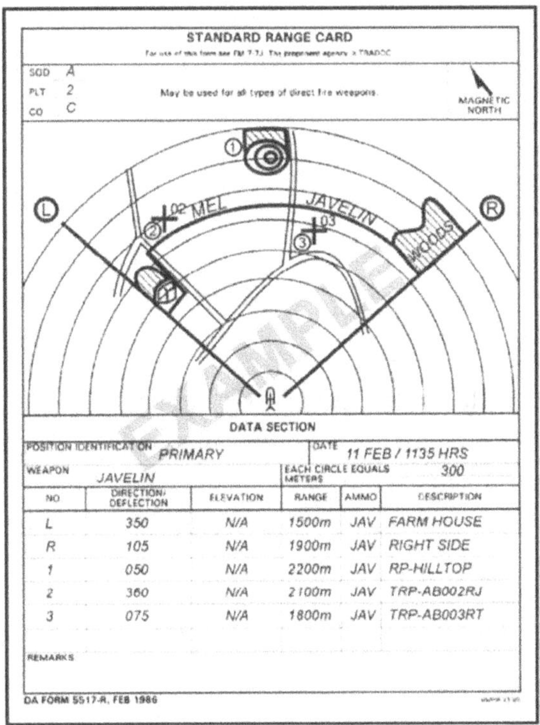

Figure 6-26. Example completed range card.

(Department of the Army 2024)

This military concept is similar to navigational buoys on waterways. Consider the space between the red and green buoys that guide ships in and out of ports and canals. They are wide enough to allow for some independent thinking based on the circumstances. These boundaries give team members the freedom to act, make decisions, and execute tasks within a defined operational space. Leaders can set the conditions for success by using standards as minimums and guidelines to maintain consistently high expectations, while allowing the team to make decisions and act within those boundaries that best fit their situation. Your team members will need the ability to adapt to situations beyond their control, and standards can enable that. This principle applies in business as much as on the battlefield. It helps reduce micromanagement while reinforcing alignment to a broader intent.

"We're not telling them every step—they're staying in the channel between the buoys. Inside that channel, they have the autonomy to choose the best path." Andrew

Standards and Trust Go Hand-in-Hand

Trust and standards are not opposing ideas; they're mutually reinforcing. When people understand the standard and see that it's applied consistently, they trust the system and each other more deeply. You can't just show up and say, 'Trust me." You build trust over time, and that trust is either built or eroded with every action, no matter how insignificant it may seem.

If a leader sets a standard—like picking up trash in the parking lot—but walks past litter themselves, they lose credibility. If a new hire is punished for missing a meeting they weren't told about, the organization undermines its own effectiveness. Standards must be deliberately communicated and consistently enforced.

> ## Leadership in Action: Andrew- When Standards Matter Most
>
> *I remember running a machine gun range in Germany, and there was one detail that could make all the difference between a safe training event and a catastrophic injury—the barrel adapter for firing blank training rounds. If it wasn't removed properly before live fire, it could cause serious injury.*
>
> *So we set a clear standard: before any live rounds were fired, a senior NCO would physically check every single weapon. No assumptions. No shortcuts.*
>
> *We had no issues. No adapters were blown off. Nobody got hurt. But the very next company didn't follow that process, and they did have an incident.*
>
> *Standards mitigate risk. When lives or livelihoods are on the line, there's no room for guesswork. You either set the standard, or you leave people vulnerable.*

Simple Standards That Empower Teams

Great leaders don't rely on complicated systems to drive results; they create clarity through simple, repeatable standards. Standards are not rules for control; they are agreements that protect time, build trust, and empower people to perform. When done right, they become the invisible framework that allows initiative and creativity to thrive.

There are many examples of easy to implement standards such as "Always leave the worksite better than you found it", "One voice in front of the customer", "Anyone can spend up to $500 to solve a customer's problem", and "If you see it, solve it".

Here are two standards with explanations that any leader can implement, simple enough to start today yet powerful enough to transform a culture.

1. Start on Time, End on Purpose

Standard: *Every meeting starts at the scheduled time and ends when the objective is achieved, not when the clock runs out.*

One of the clearest reflections of a team's discipline is how it handles time. Leaders who let meetings drift send a signal that standards are negotiable. Those who start on time and finish with purpose communicate the opposite: that time is valuable, and objectives matter.

When a manufacturing client adopted this standard, they began each daily huddle at 0800 sharp. Within a week, everyone was early. Within a month, their average meeting length dropped from 45 minutes to 20 minutes as they focused on solving, not talking. Ending early became a badge of honor, proof that preparation and clarity pay off.

Implementation tip: Publish start times, appoint a timekeeper, and close each meeting with a clear statement of decision and next steps. People will quickly adapt when they see consistency.

2. Train the Replacement

Standard: *Everyone is responsible for training the person who could do their job tomorrow.*

In the military, the best units never depended on a single individual. Anyone could step up if someone went down. In business, this same mindset turns average organizations into resilient ones.

When every team member takes ownership of teaching and documenting what they know, they build depth and confidence across the organization. It eliminates fear of absence and fosters a culture where knowledge is shared, not hoarded. It also sends a powerful message: *We promote from within because we prepare people to lead.*

Implementation tip: Pair each employee with an understudy for at least one key task. Rotate roles quarterly and review what was learned during team meetings.

The most effective standards are simple, visible, and universal. When leaders clarify expectations, they don't restrict people; they release them to perform with confidence. That's how great teams move from chaos to command.

Leaders Have the Right to Change Standards—Not to Ignore Them

There is an important leadership distinction: you can change a standard when new information or context warrants it—but you can't ignore it. Ignoring a standard signals that expectations are optional, enforcement is inconsistent, and accountability depends on mood or convenience. Changing a standard requires deliberate communication, clear reasoning, and visible follow-through. When leaders acknowledge that a standard no longer fits the situation and intentionally adjust it, they reinforce trust by demonstrating judgment, transparency, and respect for their team. Teams don't lose confidence when standards evolve; they lose confidence when standards exist on paper but disappear in practice.

For example, a team may have a standard that all decisions affecting customers require department head review before release. Under normal conditions, that standard protects quality and consistency. When time pressure increases—such as during a system outage or urgent customer crisis—a leader may temporarily adjust the standard by empowering a specific role to make decisions without the usual review. The moment of trust-building comes when the leader clearly communicates the change, defines the limits, and states when the original standard will be restored. When leaders quietly or selectively bypass the standard, teams see favoritism or chaos. When leaders intentionally adjust it, teams see clarity and confidence.

Key Principle:

Clear standards build trust. Trust builds teams. Teams win.

Leaders must clearly communicate standards. Clarity prevents confusion, resentment, and failure.

Leader Reflection Questions:

1. Have I clearly communicated the performance standards my team is expected to meet? Or am I relying on assumptions?
2. Do I model the same standards I expect from others? Are there any gaps between my words and actions?
3. How often do I hear questions like "What do you want?" or "What's expected?" from my team? What does that indicate?
4. Do I empower my team to make decisions within defined boundaries—or do I tend to micromanage?
5. What is the balance in my organization between structure (standards) and autonomy (trust)?

Team Discussion Prompts:

1. What are some examples of clearly communicated standards we follow well? What makes them effective?
2. In what areas of our work do we still experience ambiguity about what "right" looks like?
3. How does having clear standards impact how confident we feel making decisions independently?
4. Are our team's standards consistently enforced by all supervisors and leaders? Why or why not?
5. Do we view standards as tools for control or as a framework for empowerment? Why?

Chapter Three

Leadership Presence and the Power of Showing Up

Leadership isn't just what you say, it's where you are. It's showing up, listening, and making your presence felt when it matters most. One of the most overlooked but powerful aspects of leadership is communication through presence.

"Where there is friction, you apply leadership."

Col (R) Whit Wright

Communication: More Than Words

One of the most common struggles we hear from business owners is communication. People assume it's about emails, meetings, or polished presentations. But communication is far more than just message delivery; it's about message *receipt*.

The truth is, a leader might think they communicated, but unless the message is heard, understood, and internalized, it didn't land. Saying, "Well, they should have known," isn't leadership; it's an excuse. You don't get credit for broadcasting. You get credit when your people receive, understand, and act.

Presence Speaks Louder Than Email

Leadership presence doesn't always require a speech or a plan. Sometimes, it's just being physically present. When you show up on the shop floor, in the warehouse, or on the job site, you signal what's important. You show your team that you're invested, attentive, and available. It also shows you value their time by not always having them come to you.

Whether you're solving a problem or simply observing, you're casting a vote with your time. Just like a checkbook reflects your financial values, your calendar reveals your leadership priorities.

In the Army, we called this *trooping the line*. It meant walking around the perimeter to each fighting position, checking on the soldiers, seeing how they were doing. Sometimes we asked about their gear, the mission, or their guard shift. Other times, we asked if they'd called home or received a care package. These were moments of casual but powerful connection.

And it's not just a military thing. In lean manufacturing, it's called a *Gemba walk*, a practice from the Toyota Production System. (Liker 2021) Leaders go to the place where value is created, observe the process, and talk to the people doing the work. Whether you're in combat boots or steel-toe shoes, the principle is the same: go to where the work is happening. It will help you understand the reality and not just what you see in the reports and presentations. It will also help your team understand the priorities, understand why they are doing things, and ultimately build trust in you and the organization.

It's easy to say "people are our most important asset." But does your time reflect that? Does your budget?

If your calendar is full of back-to-back meetings and not a minute spent with frontline employees, you're sending a message, whether you intend to or not. If you talk about employee development but invest nothing in training, people notice.

Your calendar dictates your presence in different locations. Be mindful that your presence reflects what you prioritize. Just like what you and the company spend money on. As a leader, you must be deliberate with your calendar and checkbook. You are communicating to your team what the priorities are.

One of our mentors used to say, *"Where there is friction, apply leadership."* That's presence with a purpose. You know the project launch will be tough? Go. You sense interdepartmental tension? Show up. Is your team nervous about a new system? Be there. Your presence reinforces priorities and relieves pressure.

> ## *Leadership in Action: Andrew- Value of the Informal*
>
> *Before airborne operations, we had a ritual called "Copenhagen and informal Counseling." After final safety checks but before boarding the aircraft, we had a waiting window. During that time, we walked among our paratroopers, asked how they were doing, talked about their families, upcoming promotions, or simply joked around.*
>
> *Mixed in with these relaxed chats were reminders of the mission, checks for clarity, and subtle leadership nudges. These moments built trust, approachability, and understanding in ways no formal briefing ever could.*
>
> *In business, you can do the same. You don't need a meeting to lead. Walk through your factory floor and ask how things are going. Talk to your people. See what's working, and what's not. It's amazing what you'll learn when you just show up and ask.*

It's not about micromanagement. It's about bringing assets, insight, and support to where they're most needed. One of the most powerful leadership tools isn't a PowerPoint or a process; it's a conversation.

Don't Rely on Flowcharts—Follow the Product

Leadership presence also clarifies reality. That flowchart you reviewed in a meeting might not reflect how things really work. Walk the line. Follow the product. Talk to the people at each step. You may find the forklift drops off materials somewhere else. You may find that processes were adjusted to deal with breakdowns or delays. The only way to know is to be there.

Leadership presence makes communication real. It bridges the gap between plan and execution. Show up before the crisis. Do not wait until things go wrong to show up. If your presence only appears during reprimands and catastrophes, your team will start to dread it.

We've seen the power of presence in moments of high stress. After a platoon returned from an IED strike, Craig made sure to be in the motor pool when the patrol returned. Not with a solution, just with support. A cup of coffee, or a quiet moment, is sometimes all that is needed. Presence communicates support when words may fall short.

Similarly, if you're launching a new process or installing new equipment, don't just delegate. Show up. Stand in the background. Ask how it's going. It matters. You can be there and not micromanage but be available if there are resources needed from you.

Because when you ask your team for something hard, working late, taking on a challenge, solving a problem. They'll remember who showed up for them.

Strategic Leadership Starts with Tactical Presence

We often say leadership isn't rocket science. But it is deliberate. Presence is a critical, deliberate act. You show people what matters to you. You build trust before the emergency. You solve problems before they cascade.

And, as you empower your teams and build their capacity, you free yourself up to work on more strategic problems. You're not needed in the weeds because your people are thriving. But that only happens when you've been present, connected, and invested all along. Leadership presence is an investment. Make it count.

Communication Empowers

The success of any organization hinges on its leaders' capacity to communicate effectively and be present when it matters the most.

Leaders who communicate clearly get better results. Their teams know what to do, why it matters, and how they fit in. That clarity drives performance and morale. It is not enough to merely provide task requirements; leaders must also illuminate the overarching intent and purpose behind them. When team members understand the "why" behind their tasks, they develop a deeper sense of purpose and motivation.

Empowering team members with both knowledge and purpose equips them to anticipate obstacles and share relevant information with the right personnel. This enables them to make astute decisions that optimize results for the entire organization. In any organization, it is not always feasible for everyone to possess the same level of information or comprehension as leaders or other departments. Therefore, articulating the purpose behind each task is a critical aspect of aligning every employee's decision-making process with the higher strategy.

When employees understand how their work contributes to broader goals and objectives, they become more engaged and motivated. This unified approach ensures that the organization works together to achieve shared outcomes. Effective leaders create a culture where the purpose is clearly and consistently communicated, fostering a sense of belonging and commitment among team members at all levels.

What You Say And How You Say It Matters

As important as presence and purpose are in communication, what you say can be just as critical. To know what to say is important but the key is usually we must first listen. Only after we listen closely to discover the root cause, can we begin to apply the appropriate communication methods and techniques to transmit the solution or options at hand. How we transmit our thoughts and guidance can have a significant impact on our team's ability and desire to achieve their objectives. Not only do we have to share our purpose and reasoning with our team, but it must also be done effectively, where the message is accurately received. As leaders we must adapt to the situation given and ensure our team understands all communications.

Active Listening: The Key to Understanding

As leaders, listening to our teams is just as important as ensuring they understand our goals. Active listening involves genuinely comprehending the messages team members convey. It requires taking the time not only to listen but also to ask follow-up questions and seek different perspectives. Active listening goes beyond passive hearing; it involves fully engaging with what is being said, both verbally and non-verbally. Sometimes you just need to look up from the keyboard or put down your phone to be engaged and truly listen. When leaders prioritize active listening, they create an environment of trust, respect, and open communication. By valuing and acknowledging team members' input, leaders foster stronger connections and a deeper understanding within their teams.

Choosing the Right Communication Method

It is essential to recognize that one form of communication does not fit all situations. While some situations may warrant an email, others may be better addressed through a phone call or a face-to-face meeting. However, organizations often overlook these possibilities and default to their usual communication methods. Effective leaders understand the importance of adapting communication methods to suit the situation and the preferences of their team members. By utilizing diverse communication channels and meeting people where they are, leaders build stronger connections and ensure effective information exchange. A flexible and adaptable approach to communication fosters a culture of collaboration, innovation, and inclusivity. In addition to using the correct medium, different situations and team dynamics may call for varying leadership styles. Engaging leaders understand this and adapt their leadership approach accordingly. They may employ a democratic style, involving team members in decision-making processes and valuing their input. Alternatively, in situations requiring quick and decisive action, a more authoritative style may be necessary.

Leadership in Action: Craig- The Night the Radios Failed

There was a time during a field exercise when I was leading a company through a complex nighttime training mission. We had rehearsed every detail—routes, timelines, contingencies. But as Murphy's Law would have it, about halfway through the mission, our radio communications with one of the platoons failed. No updates. No reports. Just silence in the dark.

Now, in a high-stress situation like that, panic or micromanagement could easily take over. But I didn't need to do either. Because before that mission ever began, I had spent time explaining the bigger picture. I didn't just give tasks. I gave purpose, intent, and boundaries. The platoon leaders knew the "why" behind the mission. They understood the end state and the flexibility they had to adapt. So instead of freezing, they pushed through the objective and executed with initiative.

Eventually, we reestablished contact. They were already at the link-up point—on time and on target.

That mission showed me the results of building trust in the team. Not because everything went perfectly, but because I didn't need to control everything. I had been present where it mattered most: in the planning, in the communication, and in building trust ahead of time. Purpose did the heavy lifting when technology failed. And that's what leadership is about: communicating purpose and plans before the crisis, so your people can act with confidence during it.

By understanding and embracing different leadership styles, leaders can effectively motivate and inspire their teams, depending on the circumstances.

Leaders must choose the most suitable communication method for each scenario, whether it's a face-to-face meeting, email, phone call, or other digital tools. By making themselves accessible to their team members and communicating in ways that work best for them, leaders foster a culture of open dialogue and collaboration.

 Approachability and adaptability are key attributes of engaging leaders who build trust, encourage feedback, and create an environment where everyone's voice is valued. Leaders should be open to feedback and willing to adjust their communication style to better connect with their teams.

Communication is a two-way street that requires leaders to listen and understand their team members

---

Being present goes beyond physical presence; it encompasses being mentally and emotionally engaged with the team and the tasks at hand. Effective leaders understand the importance of being present during times of adversity and challenges. When leaders are actively engaged, they set the tone for their teams and inspire confidence and trust. Presence during challenging times demonstrates commitment, empathy, and support, which are crucial for maintaining team morale and fostering resilience. By showing up, leaders create a culture where everyone understands that they are valued and that their contributions are essential.

To achieve effective leadership, it is crucial to master the art of communication and presence. By illuminating purpose, actively listening, and adapting communication methods, leaders can make a lasting impact on their organizations. Effective leaders understand that communication is a powerful tool that empowers teams, aligns corporate strategy, and cultivates a collaborative environment. By being present during times of adversity, leaders demonstrate their commitment and inspire their teams to overcome challenges. Let us strive to be leaders who communicate with purpose, foster engagement, and inspire greatness in those we lead. Through continuous learning and practice, we can become leaders who leave a positive and lasting legacy.

The Keys to Effective Communication

Communication is the most powerful leadership tool you have. Every meeting, message, or conversation is an opportunity to shape culture, inspire action, and build trust. Yet the difference between leaders who speak and leaders who connect often comes down to five essential habits.

These are the *Keys to Effective Communication.*

1. Clarify Your Message

Every great conversation starts with clarity.
Before you speak, write, or step into a meeting, define exactly what you want to say—and why it matters. What's the central idea you want your audience to walk away with? Strip it down until it's unmistakable.

Clarity is leadership's first act of respect. When you're concise, people know you value their time. When you explain *why* something matters, you invite them into the purpose behind your message. Use plain language. Avoid jargon. Speak as if you're explaining it to someone new to the organization, because clarity benefits everyone. And never end without direction. A strong message closes with a call to action:

"Here's what we'll do next." Communication without clarity is noise; communication with purpose becomes movement.

2. Adapt to Your Audience

The most skilled communicators don't just speak, they *translate*. They understand that every audience has its own rhythm, background, and bandwidth. The way you explain a new strategy to your executive team should differ from how you present it to frontline employees or a group of new hires.

Start by reading the room. Consider the experience level, role, and emotional temperature of your listeners. Adjust your tone, formality, and level of technical detail so your message meets people where they are.

Then, bring your point to life through examples. A story, a metaphor, or a real-world analogy makes abstract ideas tangible. When you adapt your message to your audience, you're not diluting it, you're making it land.

3. Structure for Clarity

Even the best ideas get lost without structure.
Think of structure as your communication scaffolding—it holds everything together so your audience can follow without effort. Start with the headline: *What's the key idea?* Then unpack your supporting points logically, building toward action.

A simple, effective structure is **Why – What – How – Next.**

- **Why:** Begin with purpose. Why should this matter to them?

- **What:** State the main idea clearly and confidently.

- **How:** Explain the process or reasoning that supports it.

- **Next:** End with the step forward or desired outcome.

When your thoughts are organized, your audience doesn't have to work to find your meaning. You've done that work for them and that's what turns communication into leadership.

4. Encourage Two-Way Communication

True communication isn't a one-way street it's a loop.
Great leaders don't just deliver messages; they create space for dialogue. They listen as intentionally as they speak.

Ask open-ended questions. Invite perspectives. Make it clear that feedback isn't a threat, it's a strength. A simple phrase like *"What do you need from me?"* can unlock insights you'd never hear otherwise.

Foster psychological safety in your team. People speak honestly only when they know their voice won't be punished. When your team feels safe to disagree, ask questions, or share ideas, you've built the foundation for trust, innovation, and problem-solving.

Two-way communication transforms a message into a conversation and conversations create alignment.

5. Follow Up

The best communicators don't stop at "send." They circle back. Follow-up turns good communication into lasting connection.

After a meeting, summarize the key points and next steps in writing. Provide any resources or context people need to take action. A brief follow-up email shows accountability, reinforces clarity, and reduces confusion.

Then, check in. Ask if your message made sense, if questions remain, or if additional support is needed. Communication is not complete until understanding is confirmed.

Follow-through is how you prove your words weren't a performance but they were a commitment.

When you clarify your message, adapt to your audience, structure for clarity, encourage two-way communication, and follow up, you move from talking at people to communicating with them.

These five steps are habits of trust-builders, culture-shapers, and leaders who get results.

COMMUNICATION FRAMEWORK

01 Clarify Your Message

- Define the Key Objective
- Keep it concise
- Use simple direct language

02 Adapt to your Audience

- Consider the level of your team
- Adjust tone and formality
- Use examples to enhance understanding

03 Structure for Clarity

- Start with the main point
- provide context - explain WHY
- end with call to action

04 Encourage Two way Communication

- Ask for feedback
- Use open ended questions
- Create a psychologically safe environment

05 Follow Up

- Summarize in an email
- provide resources necessary
- Check in to ensure they understood

Key Principle: Purpose is your leadership compass.

When purpose is clear, decisions get easier, motivation stays strong, and teams move as one.

Leader Reflection Questions:

1. Have I clarified the 'why' behind tasks or initiatives to my team recently?
2. How have I modeled presence in times of stress, confusion, or transition?
3. When was the last time I followed a process from start to finish to truly understand it?
4. How adaptable am I with my communication methods based on situation or individual needs?
5. What do my team members feel when I enter the room—pressure, support, or indifference? Why?

Team Discussion Prompts:

1. How do we currently share information across the team—and how effective is that?
2. What are examples of times when poor communication led to a problem? What could have been done differently?
3. Do we have spaces or times where people feel safe raising concerns or offering feedback?
4. What can we do as a team to reinforce clarity, purpose, and support in daily operations?
5. Where are the current friction points in our team or operation? How can leadership presence help?

Chapter Four

Plans Are Promises: Turning Vision Into Action with the START Framework

Planning has a reputation problem. For many leaders, the word conjures images of long meetings, complex spreadsheets, and conversations that feel disconnected from real progress. It can seem like bureaucracy dressed up as productivity, something that slows momentum rather than drives it. But leaders who have operated in uncertain environments learn a different lesson: planning is not about predicting the future or controlling outcomes. It is about creating clarity. Done well, planning aligns intent, reduces hesitation, and gives teams the confidence to act decisively when conditions change. A good plan is not a rigid script — it is a shared understanding, a commitment to preparation, and ultimately a promise to your team that you have thought far enough ahead to support their success.

"I never won a fight in the ring. I always won it in preparation." Muhammad Ali

---

Effective planning is more than setting an agenda or reacting to a deadline. It's about being proactive. You can do this by anticipating friction points, allocating time and resources wisely, and ensuring your team isn't constantly scrambling.

Leaders who plan well set the conditions for success. They enable others to execute with confidence and clarity rather than confusion.

> ## *Leadership in Action: Craig- Change of Plans*
>
> *In the military, we learned early that no plan survives first contact—but planning is still everything. One of my most important responsibilities as a commander was giving my team a clear plan, not just in terms of what we were doing, but why we were doing it. I remember a training event where everything changed mid-mission, but because we had a strong plan and clear intent, my team adapted without needing new orders. We had already discussed options and contingencies during the planning ahead of the operation. That's the value of planning—it gives your people the power to adjust while staying aligned.*

Three Levels of Planning

Planning exists at multiple levels, and they should all align:

- Long-Term Planning: Where are we headed in a year? What major changes or challenges are on the horizon?
- Short-Term Planning: What do we need to accomplish this quarter or month to stay on track?
- Near-Term / Daily Planning: What do we need to do this week or today to support our bigger goals?

These layers should nest together. A well-planned morning task laddered into a weekly goal should be tied to monthly objectives, and all of it should advance the long-term vision. If these levels of planning are not nested, you will create unnecessary friction and additional work across the organization. Aligning the various levels of planning keeps everyone rowing in the same direction.

Reverse-Engineering Success: The Power of Backwards Planning

Backwards planning is one of the most reliable ways to bring order, efficiency, and focus to time-sensitive projects. It's the art of beginning with the end in mind, then working backward to define every step, deadline, and resource required to get there.

Unlike traditional "forward" planning, which starts with what you can do today, backwards planning starts with where you *must* be at the deadline. It's not about guessing the path, it's about tracing the route that guarantees you arrive on time.

The Concept

1. **Define the Finish Line.**
   Identify the exact outcome and date, what success looks like, and when it must be complete.

2. **Reverse-Engineer Each Milestone.**
   Ask, "What has to be finished immediately before this step can occur?" and continue backward until you reach today.

3. **Assign Ownership and Resources.**

You can use this concept for weekly goals to map out your daily work, or even large projects that may run over the length of a year. Starting with what success looks like and working backwards from there gives you the ability to hit your benchmarks and have success.

Planning Is an Efficiency Tool

Contrary to the idea that planning slows things down, it actually speeds things up. Think of a manufacturing line that knows a critical piece of equipment must be replaced next year. Utilizing backwards planning for budgeting, ordering, coordinating and maintenance helps avoid costly surprises and production delays. It also creates space to solve problems proactively, not reactively.

Whether you're replacing a machine or changing out seasonal inventory at a retail store, planning gives your people time to do things right the first time. It avoids frustration, burnout, and confusion—and it builds trust. The Return on Investment is always high on utilizing deliberate planning.

Field Takeaway (Craig): "A solid plan gives your team the ability to make decisions when you're not there to guide them."

The One-Third / Two-Thirds Rule

One of the most effective time management frameworks used in military leadership and easily translated to business is the 1/3 – 2/3 Rule.

If a project is due in 9 days:

- The leader takes 1/3 of that time (3 days) to plan, clarify intent, and assign responsibilities.
- The team is then given 2/3 of the time (6 days) to conduct their own planning and preparation prior to execution.

It's simple: give your people time. If you spend 8 days thinking about a report and then ask your team to produce it in 1 day, you're setting them up to fail. But when your plan respects their timeline, they deliver a better product—and you build credibility. *See the outline on page 75.*

Planning Prevents Conflict

Lack of planning often leads to unnecessary conflict. Think of the chaos that ensues when a delivery arrives unexpectedly, the team is understaffed, and nobody knows who's in charge of what. That confusion creates frustration, leads to finger-pointing, and damages morale. Planning allows you to clearly define roles, communicate timelines, and create contingencies. That way, when friction arises your team isn't caught off guard. They're ready.

Be Agile, Not Rigid.

Planning isn't about predicting the future with perfect accuracy. It's about preparing for what's likely and adapting quickly when the unexpected occurs. In the Army, our Quick Reaction Force (QRF) had to be ready to respond to anything—from recovering damaged vehicles after IEDs to securing landing zones for Medevac. The key wasn't having the perfect plan. The key was having a plan, a starting point to adapt from under pressure.

As leaders, we don't always have all the answers. But a little foresight goes a long way. In your most common scenarios, you probably already know the three most likely problems. That's where you can start with contingency planning.

Getting Started: Practical Advice

If your organization doesn't plan well now, don't try to overhaul everything in a day. Start small.

- Begin with monthly planning sessions.
- Introduce weekly huddles to align near-term actions.
- Use backwards planning for major events or known challenges.
- Ask your team: "What's most frustrating about our current workflow?" Then build simple plans to address those friction points.

Ask your boss what's coming next. Ask your team what they wish leaders would see. Every answer becomes an opportunity to lead better through preparation. Planning is a leadership investment of time, energy, and focus. And like any good investment, it pays dividends.

- It reduces mistakes.
- It builds trust.
- It empowers teams.
- And it improves outcomes.

Planning isn't flashy. It doesn't feel as exciting as execution. But it's the difference between teams that chase problems and teams that crush objectives.

Plan to win. Then lead your people there. We trust that clear plans and clear intent give teams the flexibility to execute independently.

Leadership in Action: Andrew-Backwards Planning

Planning has always been my anchor. Whether in combat or business, I've seen that good planning prevents confusion, reduces anxiety, and improves performance. I remember sitting down as a young lieutenant and learning the value of 'backward planning'—start with the outcome and work back from there. That changed everything for me. It helped me organize my time, clarify what mattered, and build trust with my soldiers. In business, I use the same logic: start with the result, then plot the steps to get there.

Great leadership is often about clarity—clarity in mission, direction, and action. That's why effective leaders rely on structured planning methods that help turn intent into execution. One such method, which we have developed and drawn from military planning but tailored for business use, is the **S.T.A.R.T. Planning Framework**. *Overview on page 53 and template on page 65.*

S.T.A.R.T. PLANNING FRAMEWORK

01 Situation

- What is the Problem or Opportunity?
- Who are key stakeholders
- What constraints to consider

02 Task and Purpose

- What is the Primary Objective?
- Why is this key task important?
- What key priorities to address.

03 Action Plan

- Who is responsible for each task?
- What is the timeline for execution?
- What benchmarks track progress?

04 Resources and Logistics

- What Resources are needed?
- What logistical challenges need to be addressed?
- Contingency plans if needed.

05 Transmission and Communication

- How will progress be communicated?
- Key Reporting Structures resources necessary
- Meeting Audiences and Frequencies

We walk through each element of the framework, to help you understand how to lead planning conversations, guide your team through complexity, and make sure no critical step is missed. Whether you're launching a product, responding to a crisis, or preparing for quarterly goals, the START framework provides a clear, actionable roadmap.

S – Situation: Define the Environment

Every plan begins with understanding your current environment. This isn't about broad statements like "sales are down" or "our supply chain is broken"—it's about defining **why** you're planning now, **who** is affected, and **what** is known or missing.

For example, if you're addressing declining customer satisfaction, your situation statement might highlight recent survey results, key complaints, and any operational gaps. It should also identify stakeholders: who is impacted if you succeed—or fail?

The key is specificity. A vague situation leads to vague planning. A well-defined situation becomes a launchpad for focused execution.

T – Task & Purpose: Clarify the Mission

Next, define exactly what you're trying to accomplish—and why it matters.

This part of the plan should clearly state the mission in 2–3 sentences. What's the objective? How does it tie into broader company goals? What does "success" look like to senior leadership or to your customers?

A good mission statement doesn't just describe the task—it communicates its strategic value. For instance, "Reduce customer ticket backlog by 30% in 60 days to improve retention" is better than "Fix support issues."

This clarity helps teams stay motivated and aligned, especially when the work gets hard.

A – Action Plan: Create a Clear Execution Path

This is where strategy turns into steps. The action plan breaks the task into tangible actions, assigns responsibilities, and sets a timeline.

Here, leaders should push for specificity: who will do what, by when? Use SMART criteria—Specific, Measurable, Achievable, Relevant, and Time-bound. Also, consider workload balance: are the assignments realistic? Prioritization is critical. Not every task carries equal weight. Highlight the few key actions that will drive the majority of the results.

This is also where contingency planning comes in. What might go wrong—and what's the backup plan? Leaders who anticipate friction can lead with agility instead of scrambling later.

R – Resources & Logistics: Prepare for What's Needed

Even the best action plans fail without the right resources. This step helps you assess what tools, personnel, partnerships, and approvals are required. This should cover everything from where we get fuel for our trucks to who is financing the new equipment.

Think through questions like:

- What systems or tools are needed?
- Are there budget or policy constraints?
- Who else needs to be involved for this to succeed?

Once the key resources have been identified, you can assign these tasks to someone who will be responsible for them.

T – Transmission & Communication: Keep Everyone Informed

Too many great plans fall apart because communication breaks down. This section defines how updates, progress, and feedback will be shared.

Determine:

- Who needs to be informed and when?
- What channels will you use (virtual or in person, meetings, reports)?
- How will changing conditions or team feedback be handled?

Effective communication includes setting a rhythm—whether that's daily stand-ups, weekly check-ins, or milestone reviews. It also means ensuring everyone is operating from the same map, especially in cross-functional teams.

Final Review & Approval – Confirm Readiness

Before moving forward, you need a final check for alignment. Are all stakeholders informed? Does leadership support the plan? Are next steps clearly assigned and understood?

This is your "go/no-go" moment. If something's missing, identify it. If everything is ready, give the green light and move forward with confidence.

Leadership Through Planning

The S.T.A.R.T. Framework doesn't just create structure, it creates leadership alignment. It gives you a common language to solve complex problems, lead teams, and deliver outcomes with purpose and accountability.

Whether you're a frontline manager, a department head, or a CEO, the discipline of working through Situation, Task & Purpose, Action,

Resources, and Transmission ensures you're not just reacting but leading with clarity and intent.

Time management

Time is a precious commodity, the only nonrenewable resource we use daily, and no matter how "green" your sustainability practices are, you can't recycle or renew it. For business leaders, time management is not merely a personal challenge; it's a critical responsibility that affects the entire organization. Wasting time can be one of the most destructive things a leader can do, as it trickles down to impacting the team's efficiency and overall success.

The Role of Prioritization

Prioritization is the cornerstone of effective time management for leaders. It enables you to make the most of your team's time and ensures that your organization moves swiftly and efficiently through challenges. When you can clearly define the priorities of your organization, you empower your team to take the initiative and achieve results without needing your constant involvement.

Leaders must have a firm grasp of what truly matters and be able to communicate it clearly to their teams. This clarity of purpose allows everyone to align their efforts toward common goals, reducing confusion and redundancy. When team members understand the top priorities, they can make decisions that are in line with these objectives, and you, as a leader, can trust them to execute tasks with minimal oversight.

As a leader, it's vital to foster a culture of priority-driven work. Encourage your team to identify the most important tasks and tackle them first, rather than getting bogged down in less critical activities. By doing so, you not only ensure that the most essential work is addressed promptly but also free up your time to focus on strategic, big-picture objectives. Effective prioritization is a powerful tool that enables leaders to lead with clarity, purpose, and efficiency.

One of the most common time management pitfalls for leaders is over-committing. It's easy to succumb to the pressure to take on more and more tasks and projects. However, leaders must remember that there are only 24 hours in a day, no matter how industrious they are. Overcommitting can lead to burnout, decreased productivity, and the risk of failing to meet important deadlines.

To address this challenge, it's crucial for leaders to be realistic about their own and their team members' commitment levels. Understand the capacity and availability of your resources. Don't underestimate how much time a task or project will take, and avoid taking on more work out of fear of disappointing others. Overcommitment can result in disappointment, not just for you but for your team and your superiors when tasks go uncompleted or fall short of expectations.

As a responsible leader, it's your duty to communicate openly with your leadership and team members about your bandwidth availability. Instead of accepting additional tasks without assessing the impact on your existing workload, seek clarity on what should be prioritized. Engage in honest conversations about resource allocation and deadlines. It's far better to manage expectations proactively than to deal with the fallout of overcommitment down the line. Sometimes you must tell them no.

Meetings with Purpose

Meetings are a common aspect of business leadership, but they can be a valuable tool or a time sink if not managed effectively. One of the most significant time management issues related to meetings is having them simply because they've always been a part of your routine. To make the most of everyone's time, it's essential to have a clear agenda and purpose for any meeting. Likewise, do not have people attending who are not providing or receiving value. There is no reason to have people in meetings if they could be doing something more productive with their time, just because a question for them "might" come up. You can always have follow up questions after the meeting.

The primary purpose of a meeting generally falls into one of two categories:

1. **Disseminate Information:** This type of meeting is meant to share vital updates, reports, or data with the team. It's a way to ensure that everyone is on the same page and informed about the latest developments. However, even in these meetings, it's crucial to ensure that the information being shared is relevant to all attendees. Don't be afraid to cancel the meeting if there is no new information.

2. **Make Decisions:** Some meetings are convened specifically to make important decisions, often involving key stakeholders. In these instances, it's critical to have a well-defined agenda and ensure that the right people are in the room. These meetings should be efficient and productive, leading to actionable outcomes.

Avoid the common trap of holding meetings simply to "keep people in the loop." These meetings tend to waste everyone's time and can lead to frustration and disengagement among team members. To improve time management, leaders should evaluate whether a meeting is truly necessary and, if so, ensure it serves a clear and purposeful role. When a meeting is necessary, we recommend capping it at a maximum of sixty minutes unless there are major extenuating circumstances. If you find yourself holding meetings over an hour in length more than once a quarter, there are likely other problems that need addressing.

Effective time management is a fundamental aspect of leadership. By prioritizing tasks, setting realistic commitments, and conducting purposeful meetings, leaders can maximize their team's time, enhance efficiency, and ultimately achieve better results. As a leader, it's your responsibility to set the tone for time management within your organization and lead by example. Effective time management is one of the keys to unlocking your team's full potential. One of the easiest and most straightforward ways to enhance your meetings is the use of an agenda. If you can't develop a quality agenda for a meeting, it should probably be an email instead. There is no reason to skip the 10 minutes to establish an agenda to keep everyone focused and ensure you get the desired outcomes from your meetings. Agendas can shape the purpose of the meeting, drive the inputs and outputs, and ultimately keep everyone accountable to a meeting that is useful to the organization and everyone involved. *Checkout the meeting planning template on page 62.*

Key Principle: A plan is a promise to your team.

Planning builds trust. It shows your team you care enough to prepare them—and equips them to respond when conditions change.

Leader Reflection Questions:

1. Do I view planning as a leadership responsibility, or something to delegate once the vision is set?
2. Have I ever created frustration by over-planning for myself and under-allocating time for my team to execute?
3. What level of planning (long-term, short-term, daily) do I naturally focus on—and which one do I tend to neglect?
4. How often do I explain the "why" behind a plan—not just the "what" and "how"?
5. Have I built trust through planning, or am I creating confusion by skipping steps or expecting last-minute results?

Team Discussion Prompts:

1. What comes to mind when we hear the word "planning"? Does it energize or frustrate us—and why?
2. What are some common points of friction in our workflow—and how could better planning reduce them?
3. Do we use our full timeline well—or do we find ourselves scrambling at the end of most projects?
4. How can we start using the 1/3–2/3 rule on upcoming deliverables or initiatives?
5. What kind of planning cadence (monthly, weekly, daily) would help us operate more smoothly?

Business Meeting Planning Template

1. Meeting Title

What is the name of the meeting? (e.g., "Weekly Operations Sync" or "Quarterly Strategic Review")

____

____

2. Purpose / Objective

What is the main goal of the meeting? What decisions, updates, or progress should occur?

____

____

3. Key Inputs

What information, documents, or updates must be prepared in advance? Who is responsible for each?

Input Type	Description / Source	Owner / Preparer

4. Expected Outputs

What should result from the meeting? (Decisions, next steps, deliverables, etc.)

Output / Outcome	Description / Format	Responsible Party

5. Meeting Frequency & Duration

How often is this meeting held and for how long?

Frequency: ☐ Daily ☐ Weekly ☐ Biweekly ☐ Monthly ☐ Quarterly ☐ One-time

Duration: _____________ minutes

6. Audience / Attendees

Who should attend and what is their role (decision-maker, presenter, contributor)?

Role / Function	Person / Title	Reason for Attending

7. Agenda Template

Pre-filled agenda structure for repeat use:

1. Opening & Review of Purpose (5 min)
2. Key Updates (Owner-led, 10–15 min)
3. Discussion / Decision Points (15–20 min)
4. Review Outputs and Assign Actions (5–10 min)
5. Confirm Next Meeting (2 min)

S.T.A.R.T. Planning Framework – Detailed Fillable Template

1. Situation

Objective: Define the current environment, key challenges, and relevant background information.

• What is the issue, opportunity, or change?
> Describe the situation in detail. What prompted this planning effort?

____

____

• What is causing or contributing to the situation?
> List specific factors or conditions leading to this issue.

____

____

• Who are the internal and external stakeholders involved or affected?
> Include team members, departments, customers, vendors, or regulatory bodies.

____

____

• What are the risks or constraints (budget, time, policies, resources)?
> Be specific about what limitations may influence your plan.

____

____

• What assumptions are you making in this plan?
> Clearly state what you are assuming to be true for the plan to work.

____

____

• Summary of the Situation:
> Summarize the key points and rationale for taking action now.

____

____

2. Task & Purpose

Objective: Clearly define the goal and why it matters.

• What exactly needs to be accomplished?
> State the end result you are working toward.

____

____

• Why is this important to the organization/team/customer?
> Explain the impact or value of this task.

____

____

• What would success look like?
> Define success in measurable, observable terms.

____

____

• Statement of Task & Purpose:
> Write 2–3 sentences combining what you're doing and why it matters.

____

____

3. Action Plan

Objective: Outline who does what and by when. Include specific tactics and contingency actions.

Task Description	Person or Team Responsible	Start Date	Due Date	How You'll Measure Success (KPI)

4. Resources & Logistics

Objective: Identify tools, people, materials, and support systems required for successful execution.

• What people do you need involved?
> List names, roles, or skill sets required.

• What tools, software, or equipment are needed?
> Specify hardware, software, or specialized resources.

• What is the financial budget or cost estimate?
> Include allocations, spending limits, or approvals needed.

• What logistical or scheduling challenges exist?
> Consider shift coverage, production schedules, or shipment delays.

____

____

• What is the backup plan if something goes wrong?
> List alternative options or emergency procedures.

____

____

5. Transmission & Communication

Objective: Ensure that everyone involved is informed, aligned, and able to give feedback.

Communication Method	Audience	Frequency	Purpose of Communication

• How will changes or decisions be communicated?
> Define the method and authority for making updates.

____

____

• How will you collect input and feedback?
> Describe your method of gathering responses from stakeholders.

Final Review & Approval

• Who must approve this plan before execution?
> Name the individuals or roles.

• When should this plan be finalized?
> State your approval deadline.

S.T.A.R.T. = Situation | Task & Purpose | Action | Resources | Transmission & Communication
Use this structured approach to create clarity, drive execution.

S.T.A.R.T. Framework Example: New Product Launch

1. Situation

Objective: Define the current environment, key challenges, and relevant background information.

• What is the issue, opportunity, or change?

Example: We are preparing to launch a new smart home device—a compact, voice-activated home security assistant. The product aligns with growing consumer demand for integrated smart home security and represents a strategic expansion of our smart tech product line.

• What is causing or contributing to the situation?

List specific factors or conditions leading to this issue.
Example: Market research shows increased demand for smart security solutions. Previous product lines have performed well, and we've seen competitors aggressively expand in this space. Our internal product roadmap identifies this launch as a key initiative for Q3.

• Who are the internal and external stakeholders involved or affected?

Include team members, departments, customers, vendors, or regulatory bodies.
Example: Internal: Product Development, Marketing, Sales/Retail, Supply Chain, IT, Customer Support. External: Retail Partners, Tech Reviewers, Privacy Regulatory Agencies, Component Suppliers.

• What are the risks or constraints (budget, time, policies, resources)?

Be specific about what limitations may influence your plan.
Example: Budget cap of $500,000; tight launch window with September 15 deadline; risk of component shipment delays; need for data privacy compliance; limited customer service staffing during back-to-school peak.

• What assumptions are you making in this plan?

Clearly state what you are assuming to be true for the plan to work.
Example: We assume that market demand will be similar to our last smart home product launch, that critical suppliers will deliver components on time, and that our e-commerce systems can handle increased traffic.

• Summary of the Situation:

Summarize the key points and rationale for taking action now.
Example: A strategic opportunity exists to launch our new smart home security assistant by mid-September. Success requires timely coordination among internal teams and partners to capture market share, generate revenue, and reinforce our position in the connected home market.

---

2. Task & Purpose

Objective: Clearly define the goal and why it matters.

• What exactly needs to be accomplished?

State the end result you are working toward.
Example: Launch the smart home security assistant across major retail and online platforms by September 15.

• Why is this important to the organization/team/customer?

Explain the impact or value of this task.
Example: This product is expected to generate $3 million in new revenue and increase our visibility in the competitive smart tech market.

• What would success look like?

Define success in measurable, observable terms.
Example: A timely launch with confirmed retail placement, live e-commerce functionality, 100% trained customer support staff, and positive product engagement metrics (e.g., 500,000 impressions and 5% engagement rate).

- **Statement of Task & Purpose:**

Write 2–3 sentences combining what you're doing and why it matters. **Example:** We are launching a new smart home security assistant by September 15 to strengthen our position in the connected home technology market. This effort will drive revenue growth, improve brand perception, and deliver value to customers seeking reliable smart security.

3. Action Plan

Objective: Outline who does what and by when. Include specific tactics and contingency actions.

Task Description	Person/ Team Responsible	Start Date	Due Date	How You'll Measure Success (KPI)
Finalize product testing	Product Development	07/15/25	08/01/25	No critical bugs reported during QA
Launch marketing campaign	Marketing Team	07/22/25	08/15/25	500,000 impressions and 5% engagement rate
Secure retail distribution channels	Sales & Retail Lead	07/20/25	08/20/25	Placement confirmed in 3 major retail stores
Train customer support staff	Support Manager	08/01/25	08/25/25	100% staff trained and scripts uploaded
Deploy e-commerce infrastructure	IT / E-Commerce Team	08/10/25	09/05/25	Online store is live with full functionality

4. Resources & Logistics

Objective: Identify tools, people, materials, and support systems required for successful execution.

• What people do you need involved?

List names, roles, or skill sets required.
Example: Product engineers, project managers, digital marketing team, retail account managers, customer support trainers, and IT developers.

• What tools, software, or equipment are needed?

Specify hardware, software, or specialized resources.
Example: CRM system, project management platform, QA testing software, Slack, e-commerce backend, customer feedback tool.

• What is the financial budget or cost estimate?

Include allocations, spending limits, or approvals needed.
Example: $500,000 total launch budget; allocated across product development, marketing, distribution logistics, and customer support.

• What logistical or scheduling challenges exist?

Consider shift coverage, production schedules, or shipment delays.
Example: Delays in component shipping, customer support coverage during peak season, and certification timeline for privacy compliance.

• What is the backup plan if something goes wrong?

List alternative options or emergency procedures.
Example: Local component suppliers on standby, phased launch (early access for select markets), and temp staffing pool identified for customer support.

---

5. Transmission & Communication

Objective: Ensure that everyone involved is informed, aligned, and able to give feedback.

Communication Method	Audience	Frequency	Purpose of Communication
Weekly Stand-ups	Cross-functional Team	Weekly	Progress tracking and issue resolution
Executive Briefings	Leadership Team	Bi-weekly	Budget updates, risks, and milestone reviews
Launch Checklist	All Departments	One-time	Confirm readiness across functions
Slack Updates	All Team Members	Daily	Real-time coordination and updates

• How will changes or decisions be communicated?

Define the method and authority for making updates.
Example: Changes are escalated to the Project Lead and communicated via Slack or email with a 48-hour decision response window.

• How will you collect input and feedback?

Describe your method of gathering responses from stakeholders.
Example: Input will be gathered through weekly retrospectives and a dedicated Slack channel for anonymous feedback or direct comments.

Final Review & Approval

• Who must approve this plan before execution?

Name the individuals or roles.
Example: VP of Product, Chief Marketing Officer, Director of Operations.

• When should this plan be finalized?

State your approval deadline.
Example: July 10, 2025

One Thirds / Two Thirds Rule

The One-Third, Two-Thirds Rule is a time management principle for leaders to ensure efficient task delegation and execution. It states that a leader should use no more than one-third of the available time for planning, decision-making, and instructions, leaving two-thirds of the time for the team for their own planning and preparation to execute the task. The team will need time to conduct their own planning and preparation before its time to execute the task so be sure to account for that.

Why It Matters:

• Ensures that teams have enough time to plan for executing tasks effectively.

• Prevents leaders from micromanaging and enables delegation.

• Encourages proactive problem-solving and accountability.

• Enhances agility in decision-making and execution

Applying the One-Third, Two-Thirds Rule

Step 1: Determine the Total Available Time

• Identify the deadline or time constraint for the task or project.

• Example: If a project must be completed in 3 days, the total time available is 72 hours.

Step 2: Allocate One-Third of the Time for Leadership Tasks

• The leader should spend no more than one-third of the total time on planning, making decisions, and assigning tasks.

• Example: 72 hours ÷ 3 = 24 hours for leadership planning.

• Activities during this phase:

o Defining objectives and expectations.

o Gathering necessary resources and information.

o Assigning tasks and responsibilities.

o Providing initial guidance and instructions.

Step 3: Allocate Two-Thirds of the Time for Team Planning and Execution

• The team should have the remaining two-thirds of the total time for preparation and completing the task.

• Example: 72 hours - 24 hours = 48 hours for execution.

• Activities during this phase:

o Team members plan and prepare for assigned tasks.

o Leader provides oversight and support when necessary.

o Progress is tracked, and adjustments are made as needed.

Chapter Five

Decide and Drive: The Leader's Role in Decision-Making

Leadership is decision-making. Sometimes you get time to think, other times you don't. Leaders have to make decisions under pressure—when you don't have all the information, when timing matters, and when hesitation carries real consequences.

Every leader, regardless of experience level, faces constant pressure to make decisions. Some choices are small and immediate; others carry long-term consequences that ripple across teams, departments, or the entire organization. When you're new to a leadership role, the weight of those decisions can feel even heavier. The temptation to rely on gut instinct, past habits, or hopeful guesswork is strong, but often ineffective. However, there are things you can do as a leader to build confidence in your judgment and clarity in your process.

DECISION MAKING

Step 1

Define the Decision to Be Made

- What Problem are you solving?
- What is the Desired Outcome?

Step 2

Gather Relevant Information

- Identify key stakeholders and seek input
- Analyze data and trends
- Consider constraints (budget, time)
- Analyze timeline

Step 3

Evaluate Options and Risk

- List possible solutions
- assess pros and cons of each
- consider short and long term consequences
- Consider wargame or pre-mortem

Step 4

Make a Decision and Communicate it

- Choose the Best Option
- Communicate the decision, reasoning and impact

Step 5

Implement and Monitor

- Assign responsibilities
- Set milestones
- Adjust if necessary

Step 6

Gather Feedback to Improve

- After Action Reviews
- Use the outcomes to drive future decisions

This **six-step decision-making framework** is designed to bring structure, clarity, and confidence to your leadership. Whether you're a small business owner managing operations or a mid-level manager facing process changes, this framework is scalable, repeatable, and powerful.

Why a Framework?

One of our goals with this book, and our leadership podcast, is to provide leaders with tangible tools, not just abstract theories. A mental model or simple checklist can help reduce decision fatigue, guide analysis, and avoid costly oversights. Even seasoned leaders benefit from structured reflection. We still pull out a sheet of paper and walk through these steps when facing big decisions. It's about making sure we haven't missed something important.

The 6-Step Decision-Making Framework

Step 1: Define the Decision to Be Made

Before solving a problem, make sure you're solving the right problem.

- What is the core issue? Not just the symptoms.
- What's the desired outcome? What are we trying to achieve?
- Is this a root cause or a side effect?

Don't move forward until you're clear on the problem, your goal, and what success looks like.

Field Note (Andrew): While teaching ROTC cadets, I would tell them, "You can plan the perfect ambush— but if you're on the wrong road, it won't matter." The same is true in business. If your decision-making starts with the wrong premise, every downstream action will fall short.

Step 2: Gather Relevant Information

You can't lead well in the dark. Decision-making depends on accurate, relevant information.

Key inputs to consider:

- Stakeholder input (especially frontline employees)
- Operational data and historical performance
- Resource constraints (time, budget, personnel)
- Market trends or competitor actions

This step isn't just analysis—it's *discovery*. That operator who's worked the same machine for 30 years? He probably knows things your spreadsheets don't. Understand the constraints and trade-offs up front. If you're not gathering wide perspectives, you're likely gathering incomplete ones.

Step 3: Evaluate Options and Risk

This is your course of action phase. The military calls these "COAs" (Courses of Action). You should aim for 2–3 clearly distinct options— not 10 minor variations of the same idea. (Department of the Army 2016)

Each option should be:

- **Feasible**: Can it be done with available resources?
- **Suitable**: Does it actually solve the problem?
- **Acceptable**: Are the risks and costs tolerable?
- **Distinguishable**: Is it truly different from the other options?

This is also where tools like war-gaming and pre-mortems come in. In a pre-mortem, you imagine the decision has already been made and failed, then think through what would have likely caused that to explore what might go wrong. This provides an environment where people are encouraged to play devil's advocate and offer dissenting opinions. These proactive thought exercises help uncover risks you might otherwise overlook.

Is the juice worth the squeeze? "You may be able to solve the problem—but at what cost?

Step 4: Make the Decision—And Communicate It

Undecided is still a decision. Delay, by default, is an action.

Once you've weighed your options, make the call—then clearly communicate both the decision and the why behind it. From the team's perspective, a silent leader is no leader at all. They may not agree with every decision, but they will respect transparency and logic. If the decision is tough, they deserve to know the reasoning. Trust is built in these moments.

Field Note (Craig): "If your team doesn't know a decision's been made, in their minds, it hasn't."

Step 5: Implement and Monitor

Execution without accountability is chaos. Once the decision is communicated:

- Assign roles and responsibilities
- Set milestones and timelines
- Monitor progress closely
- Remain adaptable

You're not locked into a rigid path. If new information emerges or external conditions change, adjust as needed. That's not indecision, that's agility.

The worst-case scenario isn't being wrong, it's being wrong, realizing it, and doing nothing.

Step 6: Gather Feedback and Improve

The final step is the most commonly skipped—but it's where the learning happens.

Conduct an After Action Review (AAR) with your team:

- What was supposed to happen?
- What actually happened?
- Why did it happen that way?
- What can we improve next time?

Don't let this turn into a blame game. The goal is organizational learning and personal growth—not finger-pointing. This is also the foundation for knowledge management. Capture lessons learned in a format that future leaders or teams can reference—shared drives, training manuals, or internal SOPs. The value of a decision is not just in the outcome—it's in the learning it creates. *The overview of this framework is on page 78 and at <u>www.commandpostcohort.com</u>*

Leadership in Action: Andrew- Frame the Problem and Act

I had to make a tough call once about a training event. There was a safety concern, but there was also a readiness deadline. I remember sitting with my first sergeant and talking it out. What helped was having a clear framework— risk, mission impact, and values. It wasn't easy, but once I understood my priorities, the decision became clearer. Today, in business, I use the same approach: frame the problem, weigh the risk, and act decisively.

From Framework to Habit

This six-step process isn't just about major strategic moves. It's just as effective for small, day-to-day decisions.

- Thinking about outsourcing part of your operation?
- Deciding whether to switch suppliers?
- Planning a new product rollout?
- Choosing how to reconfigure a shift schedule?

All of these benefit from a structured approach. Start with the end in mind. Ask the right questions. Seek perspectives. Communicate clearly. And always close the loop with feedback.

Leadership isn't about knowing all the answers. It's about having a process that keeps you grounded, adaptable, and focused on what matters most. We believe decision-making is a skill that can be built through practice, reflection, and feedback. The best leaders have a process for decision-making, even in chaos.

Paralysis by Analysis

One of the most common leadership traps isn't making the wrong decision — it's delaying the right one while waiting for perfect certainty. Leaders often convince themselves that just one more piece of information, one more opinion, or one more round of analysis will eliminate risk. In reality, that pursuit of perfection usually creates a different problem: lost momentum.

In dynamic environments, time is rarely neutral. Every moment spent chasing clarity that doesn't materially change the outcome is a moment where opportunities fade. As General Patton famously observed, "A good plan violently executed today is better than a perfect plan next week." The point is not recklessness; it is recognizing that momentum itself creates advantage.

Effective leaders learn to distinguish between information that changes a decision and information that simply delays it. They establish a deliberate decision-making process, define what "good enough" looks like, and accept that uncertainty is part of leadership. Waiting for a perfect answer often signals hesitation rather than wisdom.

At the command post, decisions are not about certainty — they are about clarity. Leaders must be willing to make the call, communicate intent, and move forward knowing that adaptation will follow. Progress comes from action, not from endless analysis.

Key Principle: Leaders make decisions, not excuses.

Avoiding decisions paralyzes teams. Even imperfect decisions, made with intent, move organizations forward.

Leader Reflection Questions:

1. Do I have a consistent process I follow when making important decisions? Or do I rely mostly on instinct?
2. When was the last time I clearly defined the problem before jumping into a solution? Did that change my approach?
3. Do I regularly seek input from frontline team members when gathering information? What insights have I missed by not doing so?
4. When I make a tough decision, do I explain the 'why' to my team—or just the 'what'? How does that affect trust?
5. Have I created space to review and learn from past decisions? Or do we just move on without reflection?

Team Discussion Prompts:

1. Do we take the time to define problems clearly? Or do we rush to action before we understand the real issue?
2. What voices or perspectives are we missing when we gather information to support a decision?
3. When decisions are made on our team, is the reasoning clearly communicated? Or are we left guessing?
4. Do we take time to reflect on how a decision played out? Or do we move on without reviewing what we learned?
5. What would it look like for us to apply this decision-making framework to an upcoming project or issue? Where could we start?

Chapter Six

Risk Isn't Always What You Expect: Lessons in Mitigation

There's a saying in the Army that risk is always present. Most people think of physical danger—gunfire, explosions, or jumping from an airplane. But in leadership, risk is broader. It hides in overconfidence, complacency, miscommunication, and bad timing. We will use a story from Craig's deployment to Afghanistan to unpack the many forms risk can take and what it truly means to mitigate it.

Types of Risk Leaders Must Consider

1. Personal Risk: Safety of personnel—physical injury or death.

2. Mission Risk: The ability to accomplish objectives on time and effectively.

3. Reputational Risk: The cost to team morale, leadership trust, or public image.

4. Operational Risk: Disruptions to systems, equipment, and procedures.

5. Financial Risk: The exposure of capital, revenue, or resources.

6. Complacency Risk: Repeated tasks that breed overconfidence and blind spots.

Leadership in Action: Craig- The Risk You Don't See Coming

During the retrograde in Afghanistan, my unit was tasked with closing and exfiltrating a large forward operating base. This required moving hundreds of Soldiers and over a hundred vehicles over three hundred miles. All our focus was on enemy action—IEDs, ambushes, mortar attacks. Every leadership meeting, planning session, and rehearsal centered around how we'd respond if we took contact. "If we take contact here, what's our immediate action?" I would ask, and we would walk through it step by step. And it made sense; the enemy had been active in that area for weeks.

But the real threat didn't come from enemy fire. It came from a winding mountain road in the Khost-Gardez Pass.

In the middle of the night, under limited visibility, one of our vehicles misjudged a turn and drove off the side of the mountain. By sheer luck, it landed on a small ledge and didn't roll any further. Over the radio, I heard the call come across: "We've got a vehicle off the road. Everyone's ok, but we need recovery support." The calm in his voice stood in sharp contrast to the situation I pictured in my head.

Immediately, I wanted my driver to take us closer so I could see for myself what had happened and help coordinate a solution. "Let's move up—I need eyes on this," I started to say. Then I stopped. I realized I would only create more risk by passing others on a narrow, dangerous stretch of road. Instead, I took a breath and keyed the radio. "you've got this. Let me know what you need." I decided to trust my team to handle it. They recovered it with a wrecker, cleared the area, and continued the movement; no one was seriously injured.

Risk isn't always where you're looking. Sometimes, the greatest danger isn't the one you've spent days preparing for—it's the one you overlooked while you were focused on the obvious threat.

Field Takeaway (Andrew): "Risk isn't always physical—sometimes it's about knowing when to act and when to trust your team."

Complacency: The Silent Threat

Over time, confidence becomes routine, and routine becomes complacency. Driving through a combat zone at night in foggy mountains sounds dangerous—but when it's the hundredth time, your brain says, "We've got this."

We were worried about enemy actions. But the riskiest part turned out to be the road. That's the challenge with complacency; it's not dramatic, but it's deadly. And as a leader, you must counteract it. That means regular refreshers, clear checklists, and rehearsals. Sometimes even more so for the basics.

Mitigation Through Process

Risk mitigation isn't about avoiding risk completely. It's about managing it wisely. Military leaders use tools like the Risk Assessment Worksheet (Defense 2014) to weigh the likelihood and severity of risks. While it might feel bureaucratic, structured thinking helps leaders make better calls in uncertain environments. This is why we always use a framework when planning large operations or any project that has significant risk involved. By using a planning framework such as our START document or one you have developed in your organization, you are more likely to identify the sometimes-overlooked threats that can sneak into even the most well-planned operations.

Key questions to assess risk:

- What's the worst-case scenario?
- How likely is it to occur?
- What impact would it have?
- What can I do now to prevent or reduce it?

In Craig's case, proper spacing, convoy speed, and the presence of a wrecker made all the difference. The mission continued safely, but the story could have ended differently.

Risk in business may not involve mountain passes, but the principles are the same:

- Product Launches: Is the risk greater in being first or being wrong?
- Market Entry: Are you ready for competition, or are you underestimating logistics?
- Operations: Is the process so familiar that no one's questioning it anymore?
- Leadership Decisions: Do you have enough real-time information, or are you acting off incomplete reports?

Just like in combat, sometimes the real risk is internal. Complacency in safety, outdated processes, and unclear delegation all introduce threats to your mission.

Leaders Assume Risk

Sometimes, you have to make a judgment call. Maybe you're the floor supervisor and the plan says to shut down Machine 3, but you're seeing warning signs on Machine 2. If your leadership is unreachable, you make the call.

That's risk assumption. And it's real leadership.

You might get a slap on the wrist, or you might save the company. That's leadership.

> *Leadership in Action: Andrew- Know When to Delegate vs. Step In*
>
> *What stood out to me from Craig's story wasn't just the driving risk—it was how he handled it. He had the discipline to stay back, to let his junior leaders manage the situation instead of rushing forward just to see it for himself. That's also risk mitigation. Sometimes you reduce risk by stepping back, not jumping in. And other times, you have to step up and make the hard call—like adjusting a shutdown plan on the factory floor based on what you're seeing in real time.*

The risk isn't always clear-cut. It's layered, and the leader's job is to navigate it based on experience, training, and input from the ground.

- Don't fixate on one kind of risk. You'll miss the others.
- Create systems and processes that flag hidden threats.
- Check for complacency. Especially with repetitive or 'routine' tasks.
- Trust your people, but verify with good communication.
- Make risk decisions deliberately—and own them.

Leadership means carrying the weight of every outcome, not just the obvious ones. Risk mitigation isn't about removing uncertainty. It's about preparing yourself, your people, and your process to handle it. It's about having a plan for the risk.

Risk mitigation means creating systems, training, and conversations that expose blind spots. Leaders don't eliminate risk—they manage it and take responsibility for outcomes.

Sometimes the biggest risk isn't the enemy—it's our own blind spots.

Key Principle: Risk hides in the things we overlook.

The obvious threats rarely sink the mission; it's the missed details and complacency that do. Stay vigilant.

Leader Reflection Questions:

1. When was the last time I was so focused on one risk that I overlooked another? What did I learn from that experience?
2. When something goes wrong, do I ask whether it was a preventable risk? Or just something I failed to anticipate?
3. Am I creating space for my team to speak up about risks they see? Do they feel heard when they do?
4. What systems do I have in place to regularly review our most "routine" processes for hidden risks?
5. When I make a risk call, do I own the outcome? Or do I distance myself from it? What message does that send to my team?

Team Discussion Prompts:

1. Do we focus more on visible, immediate risks? Or are we actively looking for hidden or process-based threats?
2. How well do we define roles and expectations when managing risk in high-pressure or fast-moving situations?
3. When was the last time we updated a safety process or operational checklist based on real-world feedback?
4. Do we trust each other enough to speak up when something doesn't feel right?
5. What's one area of our business where we should take a fresh look at the risks? Before they take us by surprise.

Chapter Seven

Coach or Command? When to Guide, When to Direct

Leadership is not about barking orders, it's about building trust through conversations.

Too often, organizations treat one-on-one meetings like a formality—or worse, a punishment. Employees hear "Hey, let's talk," and their stomach drops. But what if, instead, these sessions became the most powerful leadership tool you had?

Intentional, recurring one-on-one conversations serve as a foundational tool for building trust, guiding development, and solving problems before they grow. Drawing from our own leadership experiences—in the Army and in business—we share a template and mindset for making one-on-ones the cornerstone of your leadership style.

One-on-one meetings are where leadership happens in real time. We've used them in combat zones, business operations, and team-building environments. They build trust, drive performance, and prevent small issues from becoming big problems. Leaders can use consistent coaching to grow their team members and strengthen the organization.

Why One-on-Ones Matter

It's not about what you call it—coaching session, counseling, touchpoint—it's about the content of the conversation.

What matters is that it happens and that it's done with purpose. Consistent one-on-ones allow you to:

- Provide clear, consistent feedback
- Uncover obstacles early
- Support career development
- Build deeper trust and understanding
- Align individuals with the organization's goals

Don't let performance reviews be the first time your team hears how they're doing. One-on-ones remove the element of surprise and make evaluations a process, not a mystery. No one should walk into an annual review and be surprised. They should have had numerous opportunities throughout the year to know how they were performing and how to improve.

Field Takeaway (Craig): "Nobody should be surprised at their performance review if you've done one-on-ones right all year."

Structure of a One-on-One

Here's a proven format we've used with great success. Think of it as a flexible guide. Adapt it to your team, your tempo, and your culture. *See the one page overview on page 98.*

1. Open with Empathy

Start by checking in—personally and professionally.

- "How are you doing this week?"
- "Any wins or challenges recently?"
- "Any personal or professional updates?"

This isn't just small talk. It sets the tone for trust and signals that you *see the person*, not just the output. If someone's worried about life outside work, they're not going to be safe or focused at work.

2. Review Progress

Move into their current priorities and performance:

- What are you working on?
- What is a skill you would like to learn this year?
- Any roadblocks on your current projects?

Don't jump in to micromanage. Your role is to support. Maybe they're waiting on a part from a vendor. Maybe the workload is uneven. Maybe they're overwhelmed. Ask:
"How can I help?"

Often, leaders can remove barriers with minimal effort, but only if they are aware of them.

3. Development & Feedback

Here's where coaching really happens.

- What's a project or challenge you would love to tackle?
- What training or tools do you need?
- What is one thing you are currently working to improve?

We often assume we know what someone needs—but asking directly uncovers new opportunities. I may think someone's strong in process improvement, but they might be eager for Six Sigma training

Leadership in Action: Andrew- Recognizing Strengths and Departing from the Standard Path

Early in my time as a company commander, I had a soldier who was placed in a leadership position overseeing a small team—about four people. On paper, everything about the assignment made sense. According to the Army's career progression for his job, this was the next logical step: serve on a team, then lead one. That's the path. But something just wasn't clicking.

He wasn't undisciplined or incompetent, he simply didn't have that spark for leadership. You could tell he wasn't thriving in the role. The energy, the initiative, the presence—it just wasn't there. I watched closely, listened to feedback, and had several conversations with him. My first sergeant and I started discussing what we were seeing. He agreed that while this soldier wasn't cut out for tactical leadership, he seemed to have a mind for detail and administration.

So, we decided to try something different.

We pulled him aside and had an honest conversation: "This role doesn't seem like the best fit. But you've got other strengths. Where do you think you can best contribute?" That conversation opened the door. We reassigned him to manage our unit's retention and recruiting efforts. This new position required coordination, paperwork, and one-on-one conversations with soldiers about their futures.

It was like flipping a switch.

This soldier, who had struggled as a team leader, thrived in the retention role. He became confident, organized, and proactive. I started looking forward to our regular check-ins. Every few weeks, he'd walk me through who was coming up for re-enlistment, what bonuses were available, where we were tracking against goals, and which conversations he had lined up. The clarity and command he brought to the position were night and day compared to before.

And the results spoke for themselves.

By the end of that cycle, our company had the best retention rate in the United States Army Europe. That wasn't because of some magical leadership program or aggressive push. It was because we put the right person in the right seat on the bus, and then we got out of his way.

This experience reinforced a leadership lesson I carry with me to this day: don't be afraid to depart from the standard path. Career progressions and job titles are helpful guides, but they don't always capture human nuance. If we had forced him to stay in a role he wasn't built for, we'd have stunted his development and likely hurt the team's performance.

Instead, we found where his talents aligned with the mission. That only happened because we listened, observed, and dared to ask, "What's actually working here, and what isn't?"

You can't call a fish stupid for failing to climb a tree. Identifying strengths and weaknesses is one thing, but and determining future potential is another. Leaders have to be able to consider both and realize that sometimes people have reached a plateau and will need either more resources or training to reach new heights. Other times, maybe even a shift in roles is required to maximize their capabilities.

And sometimes, you uncover deeper truths—like Andrew's story of the young leader who struggled in his assigned role, but thrived when given a recruiting task. He turned out to be instrumental in his unit's retention success. That didn't come from rigid adherence to a plan but rather from observation, listening, and a willingness to try something different.

4. Future Planning

Shift the conversation forward:

- What are your priorities this month?
- Any upcoming challenges or big events?
- Is there anything you're concerned about?

This is where alignment happens. Your team's personal life will affect their work life—births, relocations, vacations, school, even their favorite team losing. The more you understand, the better you can lead and plan.

And it builds loyalty: She cared enough to ask about my hunting trip," or "He remembered my spouse was due soon."

5. Summarize & Sign

To close, review key takeaways and document them.

- What did the team member commit to doing?
- What did the leader commit to supporting?
- Both parties sign—formally or digitally.

It's not a trap. It's not an I-got-you. It's accountability and clarity.

This simple act of signing turns a conversation into a commitment.

Coaching takes time and requires consistency, just like professional athletes who train year round, so should leaders. Be sure that you are focused on the people and truly listening to them. Aim to have these one on ones monthly or at a minimum, quarterly. It's not only about their performance but them as a whole person and team member. You may find they have ways to add value to the organization you didn't realize. If they are not in the best role for their strengths, be willing to consider a change to enhance the entire team by placing them in a role that better suits them. This can only happen when you are committed to a two-way street of communication and real dialogue. Be willing to listen to them and their story to fully understand how they fit within your team and maximize their performance.

> ## *Leadership in Action: Craig- Real conversations*
>
> *When I became a company commander, I blocked time every month to sit down with each of my platoon leaders. At first, they were hesitant to open up and viewed it as a formality. But when I stopped trying to sound like 'the boss' and just asked real questions, they opened up. I learned more in those conversations than any report could have told me. That habit followed me into civilian leadership roles, it works because people have a need to be seen and heard.*

One-on-One Meeting Agenda

Purpose: Ensure productive conversations between leaders and employees, fostering communication, accountability, and professional growth.

📅 Meeting Date: ______
👤 Employee Name: ______
👤 Leader/Manager: ______

1. Opening & Check-In (5 Minutes)
- How are you feeling this week? Any wins or challenges?
- Any personal/professional updates you'd like to share?

2. Progress Review (15 Minutes)
- Updates on key projects, priorities, or goals.
- Any roadblocks preventing progress? How can I help?
- Are you receiving the resources and support you need?

3. Development & Feedback (15 Minutes)
- What skills or areas are you looking to improve?
- Do you feel aligned with team/company goals?
- Feedback from leader to employee & vice versa.

4. Future Focus (5 Minutes)
- What are your top priorities for the upcoming week/month?
- Any upcoming challenges or concerns?
- How can I better support your success?

📝 Key Takeaways & Action Items:
✓ ____
✓ ____

Leader Signature

Team Member Signature

Performance Counseling: When a concern has been identified.

Performance improvement conversations are one of the most important, and often most difficult, responsibilities leaders must embrace. These aren't just disciplinary moments. They are critical opportunities to reinforce standards, clarify expectations, and build trust by demonstrating that accountability and development go hand in hand.

Leaders can coach team members through performance challenges while fostering a culture of learning and commitment. We'll walk through a structured approach, provide practical examples, and discuss the leadership mindset required for these conversations to be effective. *Overview on page 103.*

Field Takeaway (Andrew): "Don't wait for problems—build trust in the quiet weeks so people will talk in the hard ones."

The Leadership Mindset

Before any coaching conversation, leaders must embrace a few critical beliefs:

> **1.** People Want to Succeed: Most team members aren't trying to fail. They want to do well and contribute.

> **2.** Improvement is Part of Growth: Struggles are inevitable, especially as people take on new roles or responsibilities.

> **3.** Accountability is Not Punishment: Holding someone accountable is an act of care and investment, not criticism.

Good leaders coach to the standard, not to emotion. That means staying objective, focusing on behaviors and outcomes, and avoiding blame or personal attacks. These conversations should be a dialogue, not a lecture.

When to Coach for Performance

Performance coaching applies when someone is:

- Failing to meet clear standards.
- Repeating a minor issue.
- Transitioning to a new role and struggling with expectations.
- Demonstrating effort but falling short in outcomes.

It's not just for egregious failure. Early intervention can prevent bad habits, avoid larger team impacts, and show that the leader is engaged and supportive.

Common Pitfalls to Avoid

- Vague feedback: Saying "you need to work harder" is less helpful than, "Your report was missing the data from the last two quarters we agreed on in our planning meeting."
- Making it personal: Focus on the action, not the person. It's about the behavior, not their character.
- Assuming intent: Don't presume why the failure occurred; ask questions to understand.

A Framework for Performance Coaching

1. Define the Performance Challenge
Start with clarity. What exactly happened? What standard was missed? Keep it specific and outcome-focused.

"The product was supposed to be released by Wednesday, but it went out on Thursday. That impacted the marketing campaign and delayed our customer rollout."

2. Clarify Standards and Expectations
Ensure both you and the employee agree on what the standard is. Was there a clear metric, timeline, or deliverable? Did the team members understand it the same way?

"You agreed in the project kickoff that the release would happen by Wednesday. Did you interpret that differently?"

3. Identify the Root Cause
This is where the coaching mindset matters. Ask open-ended questions. To discover what the real problem is.

- Was this a skill issue?
- Was there a resource constraint?
- Was the timeline realistic?

You may find:

- A training gap (they need refreshers).
- A resource issue (missing tools or materials).
- An assumption gap (they thought "end of day" meant something different).

4. Develop a Collaborative Action Plan
Don't just say "fix it." Work together to identify what needs to change:

- What support is needed?
- What changes will be made?
- Who is responsible for each action?
- When will each step be completed?

This section may include things like follow-up training, clearer SOPs, or support from another department.

5. Follow Up and Maintain Accountability
Schedule follow-up check-ins to support and track progress. This keeps the coaching active and shows commitment. Use the follow-ups to:

- Offer support.
- Recognize progress.
- Adjust the plan if needed.

Documenting this process (even informally) is useful. Signatures or notes from both parties create clarity and shared ownership.

You don't get cut from the football team the first time you miss a block. That idea is at the heart of coaching. Leaders aren't looking for perfection; they're building a team. And building a team requires patience, structure, and a belief in the people involved. Leaders have to coach their teams through mistakes, but zero mistakes is not necessarily the goal. A lack of mistakes can result from a lack of innovation or from not striving to reach new levels; this can be just as concerning as too many mistakes. We just do not want our team to commit the same mistakes repeatedly and not learn.

There is also a need to distinguish between real root causes and assumptions: It might not be motivation. It might be that one employee has older equipment that cannot produce what another machine can. He needs resources, not motivation.

When we slow down, ask the right questions, and genuinely support improvement, we not only get better outcomes but also build trust. We show our team that leadership isn't just about setting the bar. It's about helping people clear it.

Coaching isn't easy. But it's how leaders turn potential into performance.

Employee Performance Improvement Coaching Template

📅 Coaching Session Date: _______
👤 Employee Name: _______
👤 Leader/Coach: _______

1. Define the Performance Challenge
- What specific performance issue needs to be addressed?
- What impact does it have on the team/business?

✅ Example: "Missed project deadlines have delayed delivery for clients."

2. Set Clear Expectations
- What is the expected level of performance?
- How will success be measured?

✅ Example: "Complete projects on time and improve task management by using a planning tool."

3. Identify Root Causes
- What's preventing success (skills, resources, motivation, external factors)?
- Has the employee encountered similar issues before?

4. Develop an Action Plan

Action Step	Owner	Deadline	Resources Needed
Attend Leader Training	Employee	tng date	training funding
Implement Project tracking system	Employee	date	Software access /Template access
Weekly check-ins	Leader	ongoing	meeting time blocked on calendar

5. Follow-Up & Accountability
- When will progress be reviewed?
- How will improvements be tracked?
- What support will be provided?

Next Check-in Date: _______

Final Notes & Commitments:

✓ ____

✓ ____

✓ ____

---------------------   ---------------------------

Leader Signature   Team Member Signature

Key Principle: Great leaders don't give all the answers; they ask better questions. Coaching isn't about control. It's about guiding people to discover their own solutions and grow through the process.

Leadership Reflection Questions:

1. When was the last time I helped someone solve a problem *without* giving them the answer?
2. Do I regularly make time for coaching conversations, or only when something goes wrong?
3. How comfortable am I with asking questions instead of providing direction?
4. What behaviors or mindsets do I need to develop in myself to be a more effective coach?
5. What assumptions do I make about people's potential—and how might those assumptions limit the way I coach them?

Team Discussion Prompts:

1. What's the difference between managing, mentoring, and coaching? How do we use each in our team?
2. What coaching moments have had the biggest impact on your growth?
3. How can we create more space in our workflow for coaching and development?
4. What gets in the way of coaching in high-tempo environments? And how can we fix that?
5. Where are we unintentionally rewarding dependency instead of initiative?

Chapter Eight

Run Toward the Storm: Conflict as a Leadership Opportunity

The storm was coming. You could feel it in the air—subtle tension, misunderstood words, missed expectations. Conflict in any organization will eventually appear, just like rain. It may only be a little at a time or it may be a hurricane. Rest assured, it is coming. How leaders face it makes all the difference.

Some leaders try to avoid conflict. They walk the long way around, hoping time will fix things. Others charge straight in, sometimes too fast, without understanding the situation. There is a way to understand and use conflict to build stronger teams.

Buffalos and Cows

There is a story we often use when talking about conflict. It comes from the natural world. When a storm rolls in over the plains, cows and buffalo react in very different ways.

Cows will turn away from the storm and try to outrun it. Of course, they can't. The storm overtakes them, and by moving with it, they spend more time in the rain and wind than they would have otherwise. Buffalo, on the other hand, turn toward the storm. They move straight through it; therefore, they spend less time in discomfort.

That's conflict. You can run from it and suffer longer, or face it and get through it quicker.

As leaders, we must model this buffalo mindset. Conflict isn't something to avoid; it's something to address head-on. Not with aggression or anger, but with clarity, empathy, and confidence. By addressing problems early, you keep them small. Avoiding them only allows them to grow.

The Consequences of Avoidance

Every leader has had moments where they knew something wasn't right; tension between teammates, a conversation that turned sideways, a process that started breaking down. Too often, leaders hope those issues will work themselves out. But they rarely do.

Left unchecked, conflict festers. What begins as a minor misunderstanding can escalate into resentment. Minor inefficiencies grow into major failures. And perhaps worst of all, trust erodes. Not just between the individuals in conflict, but across the team. When people see that problems go unaddressed, they begin to wonder if anyone is paying attention, or worse, if anyone cares. If your team is full of cows following your lead, avoiding the storm, the whole organization ends up drenched in the downpour.

Conflict Rooted in Miscommunication

One of the most common roots of conflict is simple: miscommunication. It's rarely malicious. Someone misunderstands a task. Assumes intent. Interprets tone. Assumes they know the standard or assumes someone else does. These small miscommunications can spiral quickly when left unaddressed.

In our experience, many of these situations could have been resolved with a few simple questions to ensure we are on the same page.

There Is Such a Thing as Healthy Conflict

Not all conflict is bad. In fact, some conflict is necessary.

> ## *Leadership in Action: Andrew- Missed Meetings*
>
> *I will never forget when I got called out for missing a meeting I never knew existed. I remember my boss asking, "Where were you?" and I was completely caught off guard. I hadn't been told about the meeting at all. But it didn't matter. The assumption had already taken hold: "This guy doesn't show up."*
>
> *It didn't matter that I was doing my job or that it was an honest miscommunication. What stuck was the perception. And that was a hard lesson. In leadership, perception often carries just as much weight as reality—and once an impression forms, it's tough to change.*
>
> *That kind of situation, one without ill intent, can instantly damage a reputation or a relationship. The problem wasn't accountability. It was communication. That's why leaders must strive for clarity at every level. People can't meet expectations they never understood.*

We've both seen it firsthand—inside companies, on military teams, even between departments. Healthy conflict is the tension that comes from people who care. It happens when operations want efficiency, and sales wants customization. When junior leaders challenge an idea to improve it. When teammates bring different perspectives to the same goal.

Emotional Intelligence: Managing the Temperature in the Room

Healthy conflict requires emotional intelligence. Leaders must be aware of not just the issue, but the emotional undercurrents beneath it.

There was another moment when Andrew was evaluating a cadet's performance at summer training. When the cadet couldn't identify their location on a map, Andrew became frustrated. The cadet froze. Communication broke down. The moment was lost.

Andrew realized later that the problem wasn't just the cadet's lack of knowledge. It was the emotional temperature of the room. Expectations weren't aligned. The pressure was high. And the cadet shut down in the face of unintentional intimidation.

That's the cost of losing emotional control. It doesn't solve the problem; it just creates a new one. Leaders must learn to de-escalate themselves before they can de-escalate others.

> ## *Leadership in Action: Craig- Root Cause of the Conflict*
>
> *"I once had two team members who just couldn't get along. At first glance, it looked like a personality conflict, but instead of jumping in to 'fix' it, I spoke with each one privately and asked open-ended questions like, 'What's going on lately outside work?' I learned one was going through a personal situation at home that had nothing to do with the other person. It reminded me that what looks like interpersonal conflict is often deeper, and leaders who ask the right questions can uncover root causes before things boil over."*

From Conflict to Collaboration

Sometimes, it helps to reframe conflict as negotiation. Or even collaboration. Not every disagreement needs to be a fight. We don't have to split a pie between us. Sometimes, you want pie, and I want cake. We're not even after the same thing. But we won't know that unless we talk. Ask questions and listen well. Understand interests, not just positions. What appears to be a conflict on the surface may be just a misunderstanding of priorities. There must be time spent not only discovering each party's position but also their interests. The interests lurking beneath the surface and the unspoken ones are where you can add true value to both parties and deliver results people are happy with.

We're not advocating weakness. There's a time to hold the line. There are standards, and leaders must enforce them. But you can do that without being personal. You can hold someone accountable for missing a target without attacking their character. That balance is what earns respect. Keeping the focus on the objective standards helps prevent it from feeling like a personal attack.

We've found that setting clear standards and revisiting them often makes conflict less personal. We believe in leading with empathy, but not at the expense of accountability

Ultimately, leadership is about trust. You won't eliminate conflict. But you can model how to face it. How to ask good questions. How to stay calm. How to refocus on the mission.

And when you do, your team starts to follow your lead. You'll create a culture where people don't run from storms. Where they collaborate, even when they disagree. Where they trust each other even when it's hard. You'll build a team of buffaloes.

Field Takeaway (Andrew): "Leaders don't avoid tension—they convert it into alignment."

Key Principle: Move toward the storm.

Avoidance erodes trust. Addressing conflict quickly and constructively, demonstrates strength and care.

Leadership Reflection Questions:

1. Do I tend to avoid, delay, or confront conflict, why?
2. Have I clearly communicated the standard before holding someone accountable to it?
3. When was the last time I addressed a small issue before it became a big one?
4. How do I balance emotional intelligence with firmness when handling conflict?
5. Do I allow standards to be bent for high performers or key personalities—and what message does that send to the rest of the team?

Team Discussion Prompts:

1. What kinds of conflict do we experience most often on this team? Are they addressed or ignored?
2. How can we create a culture where feedback and disagreement are safe and productive?
3. What does "moving toward the storm" look like in our work environment?
4. How can we ensure our standards are clear enough to prevent avoidable conflict?
5. Do we trust each other enough to disagree openly? and if not, what would need to change?

Chapter Nine

Train Like You Fight: Why Repetitions, Reviews, and Reflections Matter

Training isn't just a task; it's how we future-proof our teams.

Leadership isn't just about having the right people, it's also about building the right capabilities. Training management is the system leaders use to deliberately develop those capabilities. It's how we identify needs, plan development, execute instruction, and capture lessons to feed continuous improvement.

While "training" may evoke images of corporate slide decks or check-the-box compliance, we challenge that idea. Real training, when done well, is a great tool to help your team in reaching the next level.

The Training Cycle: Planning to Performance

Military leadership hammers home the idea that training is not a one-time event but it's a cycle. (Department of the Army 2016) Below is how we like to break it down simply:

1. Set Standards
2. Plan Training
3. Rehearse and Prepare
4. Execute Training
5. Conduct After Action Reviews (AARs)
6. Improve

At Fort Campbell, Craig's unit was tasked with executing complex air assault operations, moving hundreds of personnel and equipment with precision under the cover of darkness. They didn't just "figure it out." They built up over time, from individual weapon proficiency to team-level rehearsals, all the way to full-scale execution. That progressive model applies directly to civilian organizations.

You don't drop a new team lead into a complex product launch and expect elite performance without giving them time to develop the muscle memory. Training should be incremental and based of the team's current level of performance. While NFL and high school teams both "practice football," they use different drills and set different standards. The same goes for your organization: not all training scenarios will be the same, but they should build on one another and help the team continuously develop. As people improve, the training should be increased in difficulty level to make sure they are staying at a high level of performance.

Train for the Future, Not Just the Current Job

Promotion without preparation is a leadership failure. Whether it's a newly promoted shift supervisor at a big-box store or a senior leader stepping into a C-suite role, deliberate training should be part of the transition.

The Army ensures that every time someone is promoted in rank, it comes with a leadership school. Businesses should do the same. Even if it's as simple as shadowing, mentoring, or internal leadership development programs. Without this, the organization's risk increases, and new leaders can quickly become liabilities instead of assets. This is especially important at two specific events. The first time someone is in a leadership role, and the first time they are a leader of other leaders. Those two steps are some of the most dramatic changes in a leader's journey.

The first 90 days in a new role can determine long-term success. Build a training plan that matches that weight.

Rehearsals are a Force Multiplier

Rehearsals don't have to be elaborate. They can be as simple as walking through a process on a whiteboard, role-playing a phone call, or test-running logistics for a product launch. But skipping rehearsals is where avoidable mistakes creep in.

In one example from the civilian world, a large metro hospital built a mock-up of its new wing before construction, using real crash carts and equipment to ensure the layout worked in practice. It uncovered problems before they became costly and potentially life-threatening. Seeing how the emergency room or hallway would perform in a simulated real-world scenario is extremely valuable. It's cheaper to realize you need the hallway a foot wider or the door to a room in a new place before you build the building.

Rehearsals reduce friction, reveal inefficiencies, and build trust before execution begins.

Train to Prevent, Not Just React

While many organizations only train *after* something goes wrong, proactive training is what high-performing teams prioritize. Whether it's cross-training to build bench strength or conducting refresher drills to avoid complacency, leaders must keep their teams sharp.

Field Note (Andrew) "You've got to sharpen the axe before you chop more wood." It's not about staying busy—it's about staying effective.

Too often, business leaders claim they're "too busy" for training. But when incidents occur—errors in production, safety violations, or poor customer interactions—those same leaders will wish they had invested earlier.

After Action Reviews (AARs): Close the Loop

The AAR is where lessons become learning. It's where teams talk honestly about what was supposed to happen, what actually happened, and how to improve. But AARs are only effective when blame is left at the door and ownership is shared. *See the template on page 124.*

Leaders build high-performing teams not just by acting decisively, but by reflecting deliberately. One of the most effective—and often overlooked—tools in a leader's toolkit is the After Action Review. (Department of the Army 2016) This structured, open conversation helps teams convert experience into operational wisdom, fostering continuous learning, trust, and accountability.

Below, we outline how to conduct an AAR in a business setting, drawing on both military tradition and modern organizational needs. An AAR is a structured dialogue conducted after a task, project, event, or incident to answer four key questions:

1. What was supposed to happen?
2. What actually happened?
3. Why did it happen that way?
4. What can we do better next time?

At its best, an AAR is a safe environment where people can speak honestly about outcomes, without fear of blame. Its goal isn't punishment but improved performance.

Why Leaders Must Normalize AARs

AARs help us avoid repeating mistakes, even small ones. In business, we often emphasize improvement through tools like Lean Six Sigma or operational KPIs. But human behavior needs iterative improvement too, and AARs are uniquely effective for that. They don't just analyze; they teach. Whether your team missed a deadline, nailed a product launch, or survived a chaotic trade show, AARs transform outcomes into lessons. And if done close to the event, they capture honest insight before memory fades.

> ## *Leadership in Action: Craig- Mistakes are training opportunities.*
>
> *During a field training exercise, one of our junior leaders made a poor tactical decision that resulted in a simulated ambush during movement. It was frustrating in the moment—we lost the element of surprise and "casualties" piled up fast.*
>
> *But instead of ripping into him, we ran an After Action Review (AAR). We asked him what he saw, what assumptions he made, and why he chose that route. His reasoning actually made sense— but he missed one critical detail in the planning phase. So we retrained that specific skill—map analysis, terrain evaluation—and ran the scenario again a few days later. This time, he nailed it.*
>
> *That moment reinforced something important: we train to learn, not to punish. If people are afraid to make mistakes in training, they'll never grow. But if they know we're here to make them better, they'll lean in.*
>
> *Use failure as fuel. Training should create a place to fail forward.*

Creating the Right Environment

The first time someone participates in an AAR, it can feel vulnerable. Admitting that you went left instead of right can be intimidating. That's why setting the tone is crucial. You cannot let it become a blame game, or you lose all the value. It's a place for open conversations about what happened to create true understanding.

AARs must be grounded in trust. When team members feel psychologically safe, they are more likely to offer candid feedback, admit mistakes, and share context others may not know. It's how root causes are uncovered so we don't chase the symptoms. Mistakes are okay, as long as we're making new ones. Repeating the same errors means we're not learning.

The Four Questions in Action

1. What was supposed to happen?
Clearly define the goal, plan, or expected result. Example: We were supposed to complete testing by Tuesday to launch the production line on Thursday.

2. What actually happened?
List the sequence of events factually. Maybe the testing happened Wednesday and the line launched on time, but key protocols were skipped.

3. Why did it happen that way?
Dig for root causes. Was a part delayed? Was there a miscommunication? Did someone lack training? Ask "why" multiple times to get deeper insight.

4. What can we do better next time?
Generate actionable ideas. This could mean changing vendors, ordering earlier, adding SOPs, or improving communication between teams.

Both successes and failures should be reviewed. Positive outcomes deserve celebration and analysis so they can be repeated. The purpose of using these tools are to make success repeatable.

Making AARs Actionable

One of the most overlooked elements of an AAR is follow-through. AARs shouldn't just live in a notebook or a whiteboard session. The team's observations must be captured, documented, and turned into action. This is where knowledge management comes in and the organization must have a plan to share these lessons learned and spread them throughout the team, so everyone benefits. Convert experience into operational wisdom. That's how learning leads to long term performance.

Practical Application Tips

- Conduct AARs as soon as possible after an event while memories are fresh.
- Scale the format to the situation—from a 5-minute post-meeting review to a formal debrief after a production line shutdown.
- Include everyone involved, not just leaders. Team members at all levels bring context that others miss.
- Sustain the good. Capture what worked well, not just what failed.
- Create accountability. Assign owners to follow up on lessons learned.

It takes courage to admit mistakes—and wisdom to turn them into teaching moments. You may find that the person who made the wrong decision didn't get the right report. They're the symptom, not the root cause. That's the power of AARs. They're not about perfect performance. They're about collective understanding.

Whether you're reviewing a failed deliverable or a successful sales campaign, the AAR gives your team a mirror—and a map for improvement.

Try this: Facilitate an AAR at your next project milestone. Ask the four questions. Capture the insights. Assign follow-ups. Build a habit of reflection into your leadership.

If the goal of training is improvement, the AAR is how we close the training loop and see real improvement. Done right, it reveals gaps in understanding, misalignments between departments, and opportunities for leaders to better support their teams.

Learning often *doesn't* happen during the event it happens afterwards in reflection. If leaders aren't taking time to reflect and adjust, they're simply repeating experience, not learning from it.

If you're not reviewing what actually happened against what was planned, your team may not be learning but just guessing.

Leaders must recognize that **continuous improvement isn't just for production lines—it's for leadership too.** Training management is how we keep our people sharp, our standards high, and our operations aligned.

Training is a leadership responsibility. It protects performance, prevents failure, and prepares people to step into greater responsibility. Don't treat it as a checkbox, treat it as a core part of your strategy.

Key Principle: You don't rise to the occasion; you fall to the level of your training.

Great outcomes come from consistent reps. Train hard, train real, and make training count.

Leadership Reflection Questions:

1. Is our training designed for real-world conditions? or just to check the box?
2. How do I evaluate whether my team is truly ready or just familiar with the task?
3. Am I deliberately using training to build trust, competence, and initiative?
4. How well does our training prepare people for ambiguity, not just tasks?
5. What behaviors will my team default to under pressure, and am I training those behaviors intentionally

Team Discussion Prompts:

1. What's the most effective training you've received on this team? What made it work?
2. Where do we see performance gaps that could be closed with better training?
3. How can we ensure our training reflects the real challenges we face? Not ideal scenarios?
4. IIow do we prepare people for *adaptation* as much as execution?
5. Where do we see a gap between what we train and what we expect? And how do we close it?

Training Management Template for Leaders

This training management template is based on leadership insights discussed in the Command Post Cohort podcast. It is structured to help leaders implement a repeatable, effective, and continuously improving training system across teams and departments.

1. Set Standards

Before training begins, define what "right" looks like. Standards guide every decision, evaluation, and improvement effort.

- ☐ Identify the specific skill or behavior to be developed
- ☐ Define measurable success criteria (quantitative and qualitative)
- ☐ Communicate expectations to the team clearly and consistently
- ☐ Align standards with organizational goals and values
- ☐ Ensure leaders model the standards before teaching them

"You can't train what you haven't defined."

2. Plan Training

Training should be intentional, not reactive. Use this step to design training that bridges performance gaps and reinforces standards.

- ☐ Identify the purpose: *Why is this training needed?*
- ☐ Determine who needs to be trained and why
- ☐ Establish the training goal or objective (linked to standards)
- ☐ Assign a responsible trainer or leader
- ☐ Schedule training dates and locations
- ☐ Identify required resources, SOPs, or equipment
- ☐ Communicate the plan to all stakeholders

"Deliberate planning creates deliberate performance."

3. Rehearse and Prepare

Rehearsal ensures that training execution is organized, efficient, and effective. It builds confidence, coordination, and clarity before the first repetition.

☐ Review each team member's role and responsibility
☐ Walk through the process or simulate real conditions
☐ Discuss contingencies and known failure points
☐ Refine interdepartmental coordination
☐ Ensure all logistics and safety measures are in place

"Rehearsal reveals what planning hides."

4. Execute Training

Execution is where leadership meets learning. Deliver training with purpose, enforce standards, and cultivate engagement.

☐ Reiterate the standards and objectives at the start
☐ Observe performance and provide immediate feedback
☐ Correct errors in real time, focusing on improvement, not blame
☐ Encourage peer learning and positive reinforcement
☐ Record participation and completion for accountability

"People don't rise to the occasion—they revert to their training."

5. Conduct After Action Reviews (AARs)

Every training event should end with reflection and feedback. The AAR turns experience into knowledge.

☐ What was supposed to happen?
☐ What actually happened?
☐ Why were there differences?
☐ What went well and should be sustained?
☐ What needs improvement?
☐ Are there systemic or leadership factors to address?

"The mission ends, but the learning begins."

---

6. Improve

Improvement completes the cycle. Use insights from AARs to refine standards, update systems, and strengthen future performance.

☐ Update SOPs, checklists, or lesson plans based on findings
☐ Assign ownership for each improvement action
☐ Schedule follow-up or corrective training as needed
☐ Communicate key lessons across the team or organization
☐ Track completion of improvement items and measure results

"Excellence isn't an act—it's a process of continuous improvement."

Implementation Tip

Leaders should maintain a training tracker or dashboard summarizing:
☐ Completed training events
☐ Upcoming or recurring training requirements
☐ Certifications, licenses, or compliance deadlines
☐ Key lessons learned and improvement actions completed

This ensures accountability, continuity, and long-term readiness across the organization.

After Action Review (AAR) Template

Use this AAR template to reflect on a completed project, initiative, event, or process. The goal is to identify lessons learned, reinforce what worked, and improve future performance. Facilitate openly and constructively, focusing on continuous improvement.

1. Event / Project Overview

What was the name, purpose, and timeframe of the effort being reviewed?

____

____

2. What Was Supposed To Happen?

What were the original goals, KPIs, or success metrics?

____

____

3. What Actually Happened?

Brief summary of what occurred. What were the actual results?

____

____

4. Why Did it Happen that way?

What was the root cause? What led to the divergence from the plan?

____

____

5. What Went Well?

What contributed to success? What should we repeat next time?

____

____

6. What Could Be Improved?

What didn't go as planned? What caused it? What should we do differently?

____

____

7. Key Takeaways and Lessons Learned

Summarize the biggest insights. Capture generalizable lessons.

____

____

8. Action Items and Owners

List specific next steps to improve future performance.

____

____

Chapter Ten

Leading Through Change: Adapt Without Losing Your Bearings

Change is inevitable, but not easy. In every organization, from sprawling corporations to lean startups, change arrives sooner or later. New tools, new teams, new priorities, new threats. Some organizations embrace it. Others resist it. And at the center of that divide is often one person: the leader.

So why do some teams adapt more easily? How do leaders make the process smoother? And what happens when we ignore the need for change?

Change is constant.

We sometimes say in jest, "The only constant is change." But it's not really a joke. Just ask Blockbuster or taxi companies. Or even your IT department.

Change isn't always welcomed, but it is always happening. And if you're a leader, change management is not optional. Your people will be watching how you respond to uncertainty, to discomfort, and to transformation. If you model clarity and confidence, they're more likely to follow. If you model confusion and chaos, they're likely to resist. The organization reflects the leader's personality.

While in the military, change was the norm for us. Soldiers move every few years. Procedures evolve. Units restructure. Change was built into the lifestyle, even if it was never easy. In contrast, many companies outside the military may go years or even decades without meaningful change. The longer a process has been in place, the harder it becomes to challenge.

That's why some organizations get stuck. They confuse consistency with success.

Why Change Fails

When people resist change, it's rarely just about the change. It's about:

- Lack of clarity: "Why are we doing this?"
- Fear of failure: "What if I can't learn this new system?"
- Job security: "Am I still needed if this gets automated?"

Consider the example of AI adoption. AI won't replace employees, but people who learn to use AI will replace people who don't. Just like tractors didn't replace farmers, but farmers with tractors replaced those without.

Leadership in Action: Andrew- Change as a differentiator

A friend ran a beach chair rental business. A new environmental law required all chairs to be removed nightly to protect sea turtles. Most of the industry resisted. Our friend could have seen only risk—more labor, more cost. But there was also an opportunity: lighter chairs, better marketing, turtle-friendly branding. He was quick to adapt and found his business growing due to his acceptance of the change.

Change isn't always your idea. Sometimes it comes from legislation, from market shifts, from competition. But how you respond is within your control. He was able to seize the opportunity and capture more market share based on his ability to accept and maximize change.

Vision, Communication, and Trust

So what separates the teams that handle change well from those that fall apart? We often see three distinct things that help manage change: vision, communication, and trust.

Vision means the leader can clearly explain why the change is happening and where the organization is going. If you can't see the target, your team won't aim for it.

Communication is how that vision gets translated. It's not a single email. It's time spent face to face. A two-way conversation. And when the end state isn't perfectly defined, good leaders are honest about it. "Here's what we know. Here's what we don't. And here's where we need your input." We must foster a genuine dialogue within our team to leverage everyone's skills and experience.

Trust is the foundation. If your team doesn't trust you, they'll doubt your motives, your decisions, and your process. That trust isn't built during a change—it's revealed. And if it's not there, the change becomes that much harder.

Leadership in Action: Craig- Joining Rivals

One of the units I was in was a part of the restructuring in the Army. My unit was moved to a rival brigade. Everyone initially resisted, even in an organization that was used to change. Some leaders got on board relatively quickly. Others took months. Change is a process, not a light switch. Be prepared for a deliberate and thoughtful plan to work through the change. Especially when there are other emotions involved, like joining a rival organization.

One of the most overlooked aspects of change is that it almost always involves loss. Leaders often focus on the future state — the improved system, the better outcomes, the progress that change promises. But the people experiencing the change are often focused on something else entirely: what they feel they are losing along the way.

Sometimes that loss is obvious. A role changes. A process disappears. A familiar structure no longer exists. Other times the loss is subtle but just as real, a sense of competence built over years, routines that provided comfort, or an identity tied to how things used to work.

What appears to be resistance on the surface is often grief beneath the surface. When people hesitate during change, they are not always pushing against progress. Often, they are trying to hold onto something that once helped them succeed. Leaders who dismiss that reality risk misunderstanding their teams entirely. They assume people are unwilling when they may simply be uncertain about their place in the new environment.

Ignoring the loss dimension of change creates unnecessary friction. People feel unseen. Conversations become defensive. Leaders interpret hesitation as a negative signal rather than recognizing it as a natural human response to uncertainty.

Acknowledging loss does not mean slowing progress or abandoning direction. It means recognizing that change requires both movement forward and space to process what is being left behind.

The most effective leaders do not pretend loss doesn't exist — they help their teams navigate through it. They explain why the change matters and also recognize what people valued in the old system. They create continuity where possible, even as they introduce new expectations.

In many ways, this is where trust becomes most visible. When leaders acknowledge what people are losing, they signal respect. When they communicate intent clearly, they replace uncertainty with understanding. When they remain present during the uncomfortable transition between the old and the new, they reinforce that change is something the team navigates together, not something imposed from above. Change becomes less about forcing adoption and more about guiding transition. And transition always involves letting go of something before fully embracing what comes next.

The Leader's Responsibility

Change will test you as a leader. Sometimes you'll have to sit across from someone you respect and tell them their role no longer exists. Other times, you'll have to challenge a team to adopt new tools or processes they don't yet understand. You might not even agree with the change yourself. But if you believe in the mission and you believe in your team, then you carry the responsibility.

And that means showing up and taking on your role of listening and leading. Change isn't easy. But when handled well, it can be the catalyst that moves your organization forward.

Leadership in Action: Andrew- Communication in Uncertainty

I recall leading during a time of uncertainty. The Army was restructuring medical brigades. It wasn't clear what every unit would look like after the change. But I walked down to the floor and talked to the soldiers who would be affected. I didn't lie. I didn't sugarcoat it I said: "This is what we know. Here's what will likely happen. And here's what we still need to figure out."

Transparency created stability. When leaders engage early—when they ask for feedback, when they offer clarity, when they involve people in the process—it goes better. Even if the change is hard.

Key Principle: Change is the environment, not the exception.

Leaders who expect stability are always behind. Embrace change as the normal terrain of leadership. This will keep your company ahead of its competitors.

Leader Reflection Questions:

1. How do I typically respond to organizational change? Reactively or proactively?
2. Have I clearly communicated the vision behind recent changes in my organization?
3. Do I engage in real, two-way communication when leading through uncertainty, or do I rely on announcements?
4. How much trust does my team have in me during times of change? How do I know?
5. What fears might my team be experiencing about this change, and have I acknowledged them?

Team Discussion Prompts:

1. What changes have we experienced recently, and how did we respond as a team?
2. Where have we seen effective change leadership, and what made it successful?
3. What fears or concerns does the team have right now? How can we address them together?
4. How can we improve our communication during times of transition?
5. What can we do as a team to stay aligned with the vision, even when the path forward is unclear?

Conclusion

The Command Post Leadership System exists to Make Success Repeatable

If there is one idea we want you to carry forward, it is this: Leadership is not a collection of techniques. It is a system. And the purpose of that system is trust. Throughout this book, we have talked about planning, standards, decision-making, conflict, coaching, risk, training, and change. Each chapter addressed a different piece of leadership, but none of them stand alone. They work because they reinforce each other.

The Command Post Leadership System exists to make success repeatable — especially when conditions are uncertain, time is limited, and pressure is high. Because under pressure, personality fails but systems endure.

Trust is not built through intention alone. It is built through consistent, deliberate leader behavior over time. That behavior shows up through five mechanisms:

Standards. Communication. Decision-making. Planning. Presence.

Neglect one, and trust weakens. Apply them together, and trust compounds.

Leadership has a way of revealing its lessons slowly. Sometimes those lessons come through success. More often, they arrive through friction — a plan that didn't hold together, a conversation that didn't land the way you expected, or a moment when you realized people were watching you more closely than you realized.

Looking back across the stories in this book — from early mornings in ROTC to late nights solving business problems, from training exercises to difficult leadership conversations — the common thread was never a specific technique or personality trait. It was trust.

Not the kind built through charisma or inspiration alone, but the kind that grows quietly when people learn what to expect from you. The kind that allows teams to act without hesitation because they understand the purpose behind their work. The kind that shows up when conditions become uncertain and pressure rises.

Every lesson we've shared — whether it was about standards, planning, conflict, coaching, risk, or change — points back to a single truth: Leadership works when it becomes a system people can rely on.

In the military, the command post was where clarity emerged from chaos. It was where intent became direction and direction became action. But over time, we realized the command post was never just a physical place. It was a mindset. A way of leading that asked simple but powerful questions:

> What does right look like?

> Do people understand the purpose?

> Are decisions happening at the right level?

> Have we prepared our teams to adapt?

> And what are my actions signaling when it matters most?

Those questions do not belong in a single environment. They travel with you — into businesses, organizations, communities, and any place where people depend on leadership.

We saw this clearly while working with a manufacturing leader who had stepped into a struggling operation. Production delays were common. Meetings felt endless. Frustration was visible in small ways: crossed arms, quiet conversations, hesitation where initiative once lived. At first glance, it appeared to be an operational problem. But it wasn't. It was a trust problem.

Standards existed, but each team interpreted them differently. Communication was frequent but rarely explained intent. Decisions were delayed because leaders didn't want to get them wrong. Planning focused on reacting to yesterday instead of preparing for tomorrow. Leaders were physically present but disconnected from the daily realities of their teams. None of these issues alone seemed catastrophic. Together, they slowed momentum and eroded confidence.

The turnaround didn't begin with a sweeping reorganization or new technology. It began with consistent leadership behaviors. Standards were clarified — not as slogans but as visible actions. People stopped guessing what mattered because they saw it modeled consistently. Communication shifted toward purpose. Leaders explained the why behind changes, and something important happened: resistance decreased because understanding increased. Intent drove adaptability. Decision-making accelerated. Authority was clarified, boundaries were understood, and leaders accepted that imperfect decisions often serve teams better than delayed perfection. Leaders made decisions instead of excuses. Planning changed too. It became less about predicting the future and more about preparing people for uncertainty. Plans became promises — a signal that leadership cared enough to think ahead.

And presence changed. Leaders spent less time managing from a distance and more time listening where the work happened. They showed up during difficult moments instead of avoiding them. They moved toward the storm. Within months, the measurable results improved — productivity, retention, engagement — but the deeper shift was cultural. People stopped waiting. They started leading.

From our experience, we have learned that teams rarely fail for lack of talent. They struggle when clarity fades, when standards feel inconsistent, when communication lacks intent, when decisions stall, and when leaders disappear during moments that matter most. Trust grows when those gaps close.

Leadership cannot rely on personality alone. Charisma may spark momentum, but consistency sustains it. The strongest leaders we observed were rarely the loudest. They were the most predictable in the ways that mattered. They prepared their teams knowing that you don't rise to the occasion — you fall to the level of your training. They addressed conflict early because avoidance erodes trust. They expected change because stability is rarely the environment where leadership lives. And they returned to the fundamentals again and again.

Leadership is not about perfection. It is about consistency.

Your team does not need flawless decisions. They need clarity when uncertainty grows. They need standards they can trust. They need leaders who communicate intent, make decisions, plan deliberately, and remain present when pressure increases.

The command post is not a destination you reach once.

It is a place you return to — daily, intentionally, and sometimes quietly — when leadership matters most. Set the standard. Explain the intent. Make the decision. Build the plan. Show up.

Do these consistently, and trust becomes more than an outcome. It becomes the foundation your team stands on when everything else feels uncertain.

And when trust exists, teams do more than perform.

They commit. They adapt. They endure.

Welcome to the Cohort.

Tools and Resources

Digital Copies of our resources are on our website

www.outsiders-group.com

This section is a practical toolkit — not a checklist to file away. Use the **10 Daily Habits** as micro-practices: pick two or three to adopt first, practice them, and track progress in a notebook; once they feel routine, add more. Treat the **Open-Ended Counseling Questions** as conversation starters and diagnostic tools: ask one or two at the start of regular check-ins, listen without defending, then follow up with curiosity and action steps. Read the **Planning → Air Assault** comparison as a translation guide — it's meant to show how military planning disciplines translate to business and team planning. Use the comparison to test your own plans: can you state the intent clearly? Have you identified risks and a timeline with contingencies? Put this section into practice: schedule a 15-minute daily habit check, a monthly counseling touchpoint, and a monthly planning review. The goal is simple — build repeatable practices that improve clarity, trust, and execution over time.

10 Daily Habits

Great leadership isn't about having the perfect title or making occasional big decisions—it's about consistent, daily actions that build trust, drive results, and inspire teams.

The best leaders don't wait for the right moment to lead; they develop habits that shape their impact every single day. These habits may seem small, but over time, they create a culture of trust.

Here are 10 daily habits that will make you a more effective leader. Don't feel like you have to start doing all ten every day. Pick a few that you think will help you and start there, then you can add more or try a different habit to help you in your leadership journey.

1. Start the Day with Clear Priorities

◇ The best leaders don't let their day be dictated by emails or last-minute fires. They take control by setting clear priorities before the chaos begins.

How to apply this:

- Before checking emails or attending meetings, take **5–10 minutes** to define your top three priorities for the day.

- Ask yourself: *What are the most important things I need to accomplish today?*

- Focus on **high-impact** tasks rather than getting lost in busy work.

☑ **Why it matters:** Setting priorities ensures you remain **proactive instead of reactive**, helping you stay focused on what truly moves the needle.

2. Communicate with Clarity & Purpose

◇ Every conversation, email, or Teams message is an opportunity to lead effectively. Poor communication leads to confusion, inefficiency, and disengagement.

How to apply this:

- When sending instructions, be **clear, concise, and actionable**.

- Avoid vague phrases like *"Let's look into this"*—instead, say "Can you research three possible solutions and send me a summary by 2 PM?"

- Before speaking, ask yourself: *Is my message clear? Am I providing the necessary context?*

☑ **Why it matters:** Clarity eliminates misunderstandings, rework, and frustration, making your team more productive.

---

3. Listen More Than You Speak

◇ Effective leaders don't just give orders; they ask questions and actively listen to their team. People want to feel heard and valued.

How to apply this:

- In every conversation, **pause before responding**—listen fully instead of mentally preparing your next point.

- Ask open-ended questions like, *"What challenges are you facing?"* or *"What do you think is the best way forward?"*

- Show engagement through body language, eye contact, and follow-up questions.

☑ **Why it matters:** Listening builds trust, strengthens relationships, and encourages innovation, as people feel more comfortable sharing their insights.

4. Give Recognition & Feedback Daily

◇ A simple "Thank you" or "Great job on that project" can dramatically boost motivation. Employees who feel appreciated are more engaged, productive, and loyal.

How to apply this:

- Every day, find at least one person to recognize—whether in a meeting, an email, or a quick message.

- When giving positive feedback, be specific: instead of *"Nice work!"*, say "I really appreciate the way you handled that client call—it showed great professionalism."

- Provide constructive feedback in a way that helps people grow, not feel discouraged.

☑ **Why it matters:** A culture of recognition and growth-oriented feedback leads to higher morale and better performance.

---

5. Make Decisions with Confidence (But Stay Adaptable)

◇ Leaders are responsible for making decisions, but many get stuck in analysis paralysis—overthinking instead of acting.

How to apply this:

- Gather enough information to make an informed decision, but don't wait for perfection—you can adjust as needed.

- Use the 70% Rule: If you have 70% of the information and a reasonable level of certainty, take action.

- Be willing to pivot if new insights emerge—flexibility is key.

☑ **Why it matters:** Confident decision-making keeps projects moving forward and helps teams trust your leadership.

6. Delegate, Don't Micromanage

◇ Micromanaging kills motivation. Effective leaders trust their teams and empower them to take ownership.

How to apply this:

- Identify one task per day that you can delegate.

- Provide clear expectations and let your team members decide the how, don't hover over their every move.

- Shift from control to coaching, support without taking over.

☑ **Why it matters:** Delegation frees up your time for high-value tasks and helps your team develop their own leadership skills.

---

7. Manage Your Energy, Not Just Your Time

◇ Productivity isn't just about time management—it's about energy management.

How to apply this:

- Schedule deep work (strategic thinking, planning) during your peak energy hours (usually mornings).

- Take short breaks—a 5-minute walk can reset your focus and prevent burnout.

- Pay attention to nutrition, hydration, and sleep—your brain is your greatest asset.

☑ **Why it matters:** Managing energy leads to better focus, higher productivity, and sustained leadership effectiveness.

8. Address Small Problems Before They Become Big Ones

◇ Most major workplace issues start as minor problems that were ignored. Great leaders solve issues before they escalate.

How to apply this:

- If you sense tension, inefficiencies, or miscommunications, address them immediately.
- Have quick check-ins with team members to identify and solve roadblocks early.
- Foster an open-door culture so employees feel comfortable raising concerns.

☑ **Why it matters:** Tackling small issues early prevents drama, and builds a culture of accountability.

9. Keep Learning & Stay Curious

◇ The best leaders are always learning. Growth doesn't stop at a promotion.

How to apply this:

- Spend 10 minutes a day reading a leadership article, listening to a podcast, or engaging with a mentor.
- Ask your team: *"What's one thing we can do better?"*—innovation comes from curiosity.
- Stay open to feedback—learning from mistakes makes you stronger.

☑ **Why it matters:** A learning mindset keeps you relevant, adaptable, and continuously improving.

10. End the Day with Reflection & Gratitude

◇ Before shutting down for the day, take 2 minutes to reflect: *What went well today? What could have been done better? Who made a difference that I should acknowledge tomorrow?*

How to apply this:

- Keep a leadership journal or simply pause for self-reflection.

- Start the next day with any key adjustments based on today's lessons.

- Recognize someone tomorrow who made a difference today.

☑ **Why it matters:** Reflection fuels continuous growth, while gratitude fosters a positive leadership mindset.

Final Thought: Small Habits, Big Impact

Leadership isn't about grand gestures—it's about small, daily actions that build momentum over time.

Start integrating just a few of these habits, and you'll see a difference in how you lead, influence, and inspire those around you.

Command Post Leadership 90-Day Plan

This 90-Day Leadership Plan is designed for leaders stepping into new responsibilities for people and outcomes. It provides a disciplined, practical approach to establishing trust, setting standards, and creating momentum without rushing change or avoiding hard conversations.

Leadership is not about doing everything at once. It is about doing the right things, in the right order, with clarity and intent.

This plan reflects the Command Post Leadership mindset: understand the situation, clarify purpose, set standards, and empower disciplined execution.

HOW TO USE THIS PLAN

• Complete this plan before making major changes.

• Revisit it weekly during the 90 days.

• Use it again anytime you take a new role, inherit a team, or reset after a change.

PHASE I: DAYS 1–30

Understand the Situation & Build Trust

Leadership Focus:

• Observe before acting

• Listen more than you speak

• Establish credibility through consistency

1. Situation Assessment

What is actually happening on the team today?

• What is working?

• Where is confusion or friction?

• What standards exist—explicit or assumed?

• What problems keep recurring?

2. Stakeholder Listening Plan

Who must you understand early?

• Direct reports

• Peers

• Customers or internal partners

• Your leader

For each stakeholder, identify:

• What they care about

• How they define success

• What they need from you

3. First Leadership Standard

Choose one visible standard you will model immediately.

Examples:

• Meeting discipline (1 hour limit with an agenda)

• Decision communication (tell them what you decided and why)

• Follow-through (answer the question by the time you gave them)

By Day 30:

• People understand how you operate

• You understand how the team really works

• Trust is forming through consistency

PHASE II: DAYS 31–60

Clarify Direction & Align the Team

Leadership Focus:

• Turn understanding into clarity

• Reduce ambiguity

• Align effort

4. Purpose & Intent

Answer these questions clearly and communicate them to your team effectively. Ensure they understand.

• Why does this team exist?

• What does success look like in the next 90 days?

• What will not change right now?

5. Priority Outcomes

Identify 3–5 outcomes that matter most.

(Outcomes, not tasks)

6. Roles & Expectations

Where is ownership unclear? Set the left and right limits for your team.

• Decision authority

• Standards

• Measures of success

By Day 60:

• The team understands direction

• Priorities are clear, and expectations are understood

PHASE III: DAYS 61–90

Execute, Coach, and Build Momentum

Leadership Focus:

• Execute with discipline

• Reinforce standards

• Coach deliberately

7. Execution Discipline

Ask yourself weekly, and adjust as needed:

• Are we doing what we said?

• Where are decisions slowing down?

• Where do people need support or correction?

8. Coaching Focus

Select 1–2 people for intentional coaching.

• Strengths to reinforce

• Behaviors to improve

• Clear expectations

9. 90-Day Review (After Action Review)

At Day 90, assess:

• What worked? What didn't?

• What should we sustain? What must change next cycle?

Leadership is cyclical. Clarity, standards, execution, and trust must be renewed. While this is designed for when you are stepping into new roles or new teams, the same framework can be used to continually improve your team and how you lead them.

Air Assault Planning

As a Company Commander and staff officer in the 101st Airborne Division, I learned the value of planning that directly applies to business leadership. In an air assault mission, helicopters rapidly insert troops onto a battlefield, often far from their base of operations and other friendly units. This type of operation requires meticulous planning, precise coordination, and adaptability, just like launching a major business initiative.

Key Planning Lessons for Business Leaders

1. Mission Clarity – Define the Objective Before Execution

- **Military Example:** In an air assault, the commander issues a clear mission statement: "Seize and secure Objective X by 0300 to prevent enemy reinforcements." Every decision—landing zones, troop composition, and support elements—is built around this objective.

- **Business Lesson:** A company launching a new product or initiative must **clearly define the objective and expected outcomes** before execution. If employees don't understand the goal, resources will be wasted, and execution will suffer.

☑ **Business Application:** Before launching a project, leadership should answer:

- What are we trying to accomplish?

- How will success be measured?

- How does this initiative support broader strategic goals?

2. Synchronization – Every Element Must Work Together

- **Military Example:** In an air assault, helicopters, infantry, artillery, and intelligence assets must be perfectly synchronized. If the helicopters arrive too early, troops could land without cover. If artillery fires too late, the enemy may already have repositioned.

- **Business Lesson:** In business, different departments must work in harmony. A marketing team cannot successfully launch a product if operations hasn't ensured supply chain readiness, or if sales teams haven't been trained on the product's features.

☑ **Business Application:** Before a major rollout, ensure that:

- Marketing, sales, operations, and finance are aligned.

- Timelines are established, and everyone understands their role.

- Contingencies are in place if things don't go according to plan.

3. Contingency Planning – No Plan Survives First Contact

- **Military Example:** In an air assault, planners identify "PZ (pickup zone) contingencies" and "LZ (landing zone) contingencies." If the primary landing site is compromised, pre-planned alternate zones ensure mission success despite unexpected resistance.

- **Business Lesson:** In business, leaders must anticipate obstacles and build flexibility into their plans. A product launch might face supply chain delays, regulatory hurdles, or unexpected competitor moves. Having contingencies in place ensures quick adaptation.

☑ **Business Application:** When planning a business initiative, ask:

- What if a key supplier falls through?

- What if customer adoption is slower than expected?

- What's the backup plan if the primary strategy doesn't work?

4. Logistics & Resource Allocation – Setting Up for Success

- **Military Example:** An air assault requires careful fuel calculations, ammunition resupply plans, and medical evacuation contingencies. A lack of planning in any of these areas can lead to mission failure.

- **Business Lesson:** In business, leaders must ensure that the right resources—funding, personnel, and technology—are allocated before execution begins. Under-resourcing a project leads to costly failures and missed opportunities.

☑ **Business Application:** Before executing a business initiative, ensure that:

- Funding and staffing levels match the scope of the project.

- Necessary tools and technologies are in place.

- Leadership is monitoring execution and making adjustments as needed.

5. Decision-Making Under Pressure – Trust the Plan, but Adapt When Needed

- **Military Example:** Once the helicopters are airborne, leaders must make quick decisions based on real-time intelligence. If enemy forces are present at the planned landing zone, commanders must quickly adjust and shift to an alternate site.

- **Business Lesson:** In business, conditions change—markets shift, competitors react, and internal challenges arise. Leaders must be decisive, trust their planning, and adjust quickly when necessary.

☑ **Business Application:** Encourage a culture where:

- Leaders make informed decisions with the best available data.

- Teams are empowered to adapt to changing conditions.

- Adjustments are seen as strategic pivots, not failures.

An air assault mission is a high-risk, high-reward operation that depends on clear objectives, synchronized execution, contingency planning, resource management, and adaptability—exactly the same principles that determine business success.

🚁 **Business Leaders Must Think Like Planning an Air Assault:**

☑ Set a clear mission

☑ Synchronize efforts across teams

☑ Plan for contingencies

☑ Allocate the right resources

☑ Adapt to changes in real time

Open-ended questions to enhance conversations

These questions can help guide one-on-one meetings or team discussions.

1. Understanding Their Perspective

1. What part of your job do you enjoy the most?

2. What are the biggest challenges you face in your role?

3. What's something you've learned recently that has helped you in your job?

4. What do you think is currently working well in our team?

5. What's one thing you wish you had more time to focus on?

6. How do you feel about your work-life balance?

7. What would make your job easier or more enjoyable?

8. How do you define success in your current role?

9. What's one thing that frustrates you at work, and why?

10. What's something you'd like to see improved within the organization?

2. Goal-Setting & Growth

1. What are your top three career goals right now?

2. What skills would you like to develop in the next six months?

3. If you could take on a new responsibility, what would it be?

4. What motivates you to keep pushing forward in your role?

5. Where do you see yourself in five years, and how can I help you get there?

6. What professional development opportunities would you be interested in?

7. What's a project or challenge you'd love to tackle?

8. How do you define personal and professional growth?

9. What's the most valuable lesson you've learned in your career so far?

10. How can I better support your long-term career aspirations?

3. Team & Collaboration

1. How do you feel about the way our team communicates?

2. What's one thing our team does well?

3. What's one thing our team could improve?

4. How can we create a more collaborative team environment?

5. What's your preferred way to share and receive feedback from teammates?

6. How do you handle conflicts or disagreements within the team?

7. What do you appreciate most about your colleagues?

8. How do you think we can improve team morale?

9. What would help you feel more connected to your teammates?

10. What can we do as a team to be more effective?

4. Performance & Feedback

1. What do you think is your greatest strength in your role?

2. What's one thing you're currently working to improve?

3. Can you share an example of a recent challenge you faced and how you handled it?

4. How do you prefer to receive feedback?

5. What's something you accomplished recently that you're proud of?

6. What barriers are preventing you from reaching your full potential?

7. How do you measure success in your work?

8. What additional support or resources would help you perform better?

9. What's one thing I can do to help you be more successful?

10. How can we make performance evaluations more meaningful for you?

---

5. Motivation & Engagement

1. What excites you most about your job?

2. What kind of work do you find most fulfilling?

3. What drains your motivation, and how can we address it?

4. What's one thing leadership could do to keep you engaged?

5. How do you like to be recognized for your work?

6. What gives you a sense of purpose in your role?

7. How do you recharge when work feels overwhelming?

8. What's something that would make your daily work experience more enjoyable?

9. What's one project or initiative that would excite you?

10. How do you stay motivated when facing setbacks or challenges?

6. Leadership & Support

1. What does good leadership look like to you?

2. How can I be a better leader for you?

3. What's one thing I should start doing to better support you?

4. What's one thing I should stop doing that isn't helpful to you?

5. How do you prefer to receive direction and guidance?

6. What's an example of great leadership you've experienced?

7. What's one area where you'd like more autonomy in your work?

8. How can I help remove obstacles that slow you down?

9. What's the best way for me to challenge and develop you?

10. What's something you wish leaders in this organization understood better?

Open-Ended Questions for Resolving Team Conflict

Here are 40 open-ended questions categorized into four key areas to help leaders effectively navigate and resolve team conflicts.

1. Understanding the Conflict

1. Can you walk me through what happened from your perspective?

2. When did you first notice this issue, and how has it evolved?

3. What specific actions or behaviors contributed to this conflict?

4. How has this situation affected your ability to work effectively?

5. What emotions are you experiencing regarding this situation?

6. What do you believe was the root cause of the disagreement?

7. Have you faced similar challenges with this person or situation before?

8. What assumptions might you be making about the other person's intentions?

9. How do you feel this situation impacts the team as a whole?

10. What would you like to see change in order to move forward?

2. Encouraging Perspective-Taking

11. Have you spoken directly with the other person about this issue? If not, why?

12. How do you think the other person is feeling about this situation?

13. What do you think the other person's concerns are?

14. Can you see any valid points in their perspective?

15. If the roles were reversed, how would you feel?

16. Do you think there were any miscommunications that contributed to this situation?

17. What common goals do you and the other person share?

18. How do you think your working styles or communication differences play a role in this?

19. What would happen if this conflict were left unresolved?

20. If you could step outside of the situation, how would you advise someone else to handle it?

3. Finding Solutions

21. What are some possible solutions that would feel fair to both of you?

22. What needs to happen for you to feel comfortable moving forward?

23. What compromises are you willing to make to resolve this?

24. What would an ideal resolution look like for you and for them?

25. How can both of you ensure this issue doesn't happen again?

26. What is one small step you could take today to improve the situation?

27. What support do you need from leadership to help resolve this conflict?

28. Is there a process or guideline we can put in place to prevent this issue in the future?

29. How can you and the other person work together more effectively going forward?

30. What steps would you like to take next to resolve this issue?

4. Rebuilding Trust & Moving Forward

31. What do you think needs to happen to rebuild trust between you and your teammate?

32. How can you improve communication with this person moving forward?

33. What lessons can be learned from this situation to strengthen the team?

34. What specific actions can both of you take to create a more positive working relationship?

35. How can you hold each other accountable for respectful and productive collaboration?

36. What expectations do you want to set for how you'll work together in the future?

37. How can leadership support you in moving past this conflict?

38. How can we make sure that this resolution lasts long-term?

39. What are some ways you can both acknowledge progress and improvements?

40. What would success look like in terms of moving past this conflict?

These questions can guide one-on-one conversations, mediation sessions, or team discussions to help resolve conflicts effectively.

Examples and Exercises for in-person Workshops with Craig and Andrew

Exercise: Personal Interpretation & Assumptions

Instructions:
Complete each statement with your interpretation. Then, compare your answers with others to see how differently people understand common phrases. This activity reveals how assumptions and unclear language can lead to miscommunication in leadership, teamwork, and daily life.

What does it mean to "show up early" to a meeting?
Your Answer:

____

____

____

How many minutes early is that?

____

What's considered "a lot of money"?
Your Answer:

____

____

____

In what context?

____

How fast is "driving fast"?
Your Answer:

____

____

____

Where (city, highway, rural road)?

____

What does "ASAP" mean to you?
Your Answer:

____

____

____

Within what timeframe?

____

How would you define a "clean" workspace?
Your Answer:

____

____

____

What does it look like specifically?

____

What is a "reasonable amount of time" to respond to an email?
Your Answer:

____

____

____

Does your answer change based on urgency or role?

____

Exercise: Adapting Your Message to the Audience

Objective:

Develop the ability to adjust tone, content, and style to the audience while maintaining clarity and professionalism in business communication.

Scenario: Product Launch Delay

You are the project manager for a new software platform. It was scheduled to launch next month, but due to unforeseen integration issues with a key vendor system, the release will be delayed by six weeks.

Your job is to communicate this delay to various stakeholders, each with different interests, priorities, and concerns.

Instructions:

1. Read the scenario above.
2. On your own or in small groups, write a brief 3–5 sentence message for each audience below.
3. Afterward, review the example responses.
4. Discuss the reflection questions as a group.

Your Task: Draft Messages to These Four Audiences

Executive Leadership Team

Consider: strategy, risk, mitigation, accountability

Message:

____

____

____

____

____

____

Internal Project Team

Consider: morale, collaboration, technical detail

Message:

____

____

____

____

____

Major Client Expecting the Product

Consider: professionalism, reassurance, impact on their plans

Message:

____

____

____

____

____

Customer Service Department

Consider: preparedness, client-facing messaging, tools they need

Message:

____

____

____

____

____

Example Messages

1. Executive Leadership Team

Good Example Message:
"We've identified a critical integration issue that will delay the software launch by six weeks. The team has already implemented a revised timeline and mitigation plan, including vendor coordination and added QA resources. While this impacts our Q2 delivery, we expect no long-term disruption to client commitments or revenue projections."

Why it works:

- Strategic, concise, solution-focused

- Addresses risk and recovery

- Uses leadership-level language (e.g., "mitigation plan", "revenue projections")

2. Internal Project Team

Good Example Message:
"Team, we've hit an integration challenge that will push the launch back by six weeks. I know this is frustrating, but it's solvable and we're adjusting the schedule to reflect priorities. Let's regroup at tomorrow's stand-up to walk through revised action items and adjustments to our schedule and focus."

Why it works:

- Honest but optimistic tone

- Acknowledges team emotions

- Emphasizes teamwork and next steps

- Keeps detail actionable and relevant

3. Major Client

Good Example Message:
"I want to inform you that our software platform launch has been delayed by six weeks due to a technical integration issue. We're actively resolving it and have updated our roadmap to ensure a smooth rollout. I understand this may affect your plans, and I'll personally ensure you're updated weekly and supported throughout."

Why it works:

- Clear and professional tone

- Expresses ownership and empathy

- Provides assurance of ongoing communication

4. Customer Service Department

Good Example Message:
"The new platform's launch is delayed by six weeks due to integration issues. You may begin receiving questions from clients, so key talking points include: (1) we're prioritizing stability and quality, (2) all current systems remain supported, and (3) clients will be updated proactively. A support FAQ will be shared by end of day."

Why it works:

- Prepares the team with messaging

- Anticipates frontline needs

- Adds actionable next steps

Group Discussion Questions

• How did your tone or content change between audiences?

• Which message was hardest to write—and why?

• What risks come with using the same message for all audiences?

• Why does adjusting your message matter for leadership credibility?

• In your role (or future role), which of these audiences do you communicate with most? How can this skill help you?

ABOUT THE AUTHORS

Craig Oglesby and Andrew Partin are leadership consultants, podcast hosts, and former Army officers who have spent their careers leading high-performing teams in some of the most demanding environments imaginable—both in combat and in business.

Craig brings a wealth of experience from his time as a company commander and now as a business owner, elected county commissioner, and leadership advisor. He specializes in strategic planning, organizational development, and practical leadership training for emerging and mid-level leaders. With an MBA and certifications in Lean Six Sigma and Change Management, Craig blends battlefield-tested leadership with business acumen to help leaders thrive under pressure.

Andrew is a former Army officer turned small business owner and leadership coach. With a passion for mentoring others, he translates real-world leadership challenges into relatable, actionable lessons. Andrew's strength lies in helping teams improve communication, accountability, and decision-making through purpose-driven leadership.

Together, Craig and Andrew co-host the Command Post Cohort podcast, where they share stories and leadership insights from their time in uniform and their journeys in entrepreneurship. Their work is grounded in authenticity, humility, and a shared mission: to build better leaders who create stronger teams and lasting impact.

If you would like information on scheduling Craig or Andrew for in-person training, workshops, facilitation, or coaching. Reach out on their website
www.outsiders-group.com

INDEX

Works Cited

Defense, Department of. "Deliberate Risk Assessment Worksheet DD2977." Department of Defense, 2014.

Department of the Army. *Infantry Rifle Platoon and Squad ATP 3-21.8*. Washington D.C.: Department of the Army, 2024.

—. *Mission Command: Command and Control of Army Forces ADP 6-0*. Washington D.C.: Department of the Army, 2019.

—. *Train to Win in a Complex World FM 7-0*. Washington D.C.: Department of the Army, 2016.

Liker, Jeffrey K. *The Toyota Way: 14 management principles from the world's greatest manufacturer*. New York: Mcgraw Hill, 2021.

"Giddy Up"

COL (R) William "Billy" Shaw

www.ingramcontent.com/pod-product-compliance
Lightning Source LLC
Chambersburg PA
CBHW081212130726
47997CB00009B/2639